# Whispers of the Zen Fo

A Zen Practice Workbook for Mastering Mindfulness, Meditation, and Positive Thinking to Relieve Stress, Overcome Anxiety, and Achieve Inner Peace

By

***Sati Siroda***

**Book Ecke**

## Whispers of the Zen Forest Workbook

A Zen Practice Workbook for Mastering Mindfulness, Meditation, and Positive Thinking to Relieve Stress, Overcome Anxiety, and Achieve Inner Peace

By

*Sati Siroda*



**ISBN**

**eBook: 978-81-986117-9-6**

**Paperback: 978-81-986117-6-5**

**Hardback: 978-81-986117-8-9**

First edition [2025]

*Published by Book Ecke*

*15A, 4th Floor, City Vista, Tower A,*

*Suite No.1140, Fountain Road, Kharadi, Pune - 411014*

Cover Art: Safeer Ahmed

Visit www.bookecke.com for any further information.

To Life, my greatest guide—

For every whisper of joy, silence, sorrow, and awakening.

And to those who lit the path with presence,

Your wisdom lives gently within me.

…and to Asoka Siroda—

Thank you for walking this winding path beside me,

For every quiet step,

For every unspoken promise

That we would find our way, together.

**BOOKS BY SATI SIRODA**

Mind the Quote

Poulomi's Abode of Thoughts

Coffee Tales: Short Stories of Wisdom

Earnest Poetica: Ink Expressions of the Ineffable Heart

Gratitude Journal: Reflect, Appreciate, Transform in 60 Days

Inspiring Stories for Amazing Girls Who Believe in Themselves

Inspiring Stories for Amazing Boys Who Believe in Themselves

I Am 6 and Wonderful

I Am 6 and Brave

Whispers of the Zen Forest

# Table of Contents

## *Special Acknowledgement*

A heartfelt bow of gratitude to *For a Future to Be Possible* by Thich Nhat Hanh—whose clarity and compassion in presenting the Five Mindfulness Trainings have deeply shaped the spirit of this book. His words hold the kind of truth that does not fade, and because of that, this book carries the original training sentences as they are—faithful to the source and offered with the same reverence. Without his gentle yet powerful guidance, these teachings would not have found such a clear and loving voice.

# Introduction

## *Why This Workbook Exists — and Why You Were Right to Choose It*

**The Quiet Search for Peace**

Most people don't come to mindfulness because life is easy.

They come because life is ***LOUD.***

Stress accumulates. Thoughts become cluttered. Anxiety rises. Relationships become strained. Sleep becomes lighter. The mind becomes harder to manage. At some point, you whisper to yourself:

*"There has to be another way to live."*

This workbook is for that moment. Not the dramatic moments. Not the breakdown moments. Not the "I need a miracle" moments. It is for the subtle moment when a part of you finally whispers:

- *"I'm ready to breathe differently."*
- *"I'm ready to think differently."*
- *"I'm ready to show up differently."*

You picked up this workbook because something inside you already knows…

- *You deserve a calm mind.*
- *You deserve emotional clarity.*
- *You deserve inner stability and peace.*
- *You deserve to feel grounded, centered, and aligned again.*

This workbook helps you do exactly that.

**Why This Workbook Is Different**

- Most mindfulness books tell you *what* mindfulness is. This workbook helps you ***live*** it.
- Most self-help books give strategies. This workbook gives you ***practice.***
- Most spirituality books offer philosophy. This workbook offers ***transformation tools*** grounded in:

- Zen teachings
  - Modern psychology
  - Mindfulness-based stress reduction
  - Cognitive and emotional regulation
  - Behavioral science
  - Trauma-informed approaches
  - Simple, practical daily rituals
- It bridges ***ancient wisdom and modern neuroscience***, allowing you to understand ***why*** these teachings work and ***how*** they actually reshape the mind.

You will not only read—you will integrate.

**Why We Begin with Zen Stories**

The human mind naturally understands stories more deeply than instructions.

Stories bypass resistance, speak the language of emotion, reveal our patterns without judgment, help us make meaning of our experiences, and become mirrors.

In ***Whispers of the Zen Forest*,** every story was crafted with symbolic intention, for example:

- The lantern = clarity
- The wind = emotional turbulence
- The river = letting go
- The mountain = stability
- The leaf = impermanence
- The forest = your inner world

This workbook transforms those 50 Zen stories into 50 moments of insight, self-discovery, grounding, emotional release, behavioral change, mental clarity, and spiritual nourishment

Each story becomes a practice you can live through, not just a tale you read.

**Why Ethical Foundations Come First**

Before meditation… Before breathwork… Before positive thinking… Before emotional healing… We must begin with *ethical grounding.* Not because ethics are restrictive, but because ethics stabilize the mind.

Modern psychology confirms what the Buddha taught:

- When your actions contradict your values → anxiety increases.
- When your behavior is incongruent → the nervous system becomes tense.
- When your choices create internal conflict → stress rises.

The Five Mindfulness Trainings *(Pañca-sīla)* are not religious rules. They are psychological foundations for mental well-being:

1. *Non-harm* → reduces reactivity
2. *Generosity* → increases contentment
3. *Healthy relationships* → support emotional safety
4. *Loving speech* → reduces conflict
5. *Mindful consumption* → protects mental clarity

This workbook teaches these trainings in a way modern readers can understand and apply—without dogma, pressure, or complexity.

**Why You Don't Need Experience**

You do ***NOT*** need prior meditation experience, knowledge of Buddhism, or any background in spirituality. You don't need a calm mind, perfect discipline, strong focus, or emotional stability. This workbook welcomes you exactly as you are, with the understanding that growth begins from the real, imperfect, human place you're standing in right now. You only need…

- *A willingness to explore your inner world.*
- *A willingness to pause.*
- *A willingness to discover.*
- *A willingness to be patient with yourself.*

Mindfulness is not a skill for the gifted. It is a skill for humans.

**How to Use This Workbook**

You will move through this book in two phases:

**PHASE 1 — Foundations (Chapters 1–9)**

These chapters build your:

- psychological understanding
- mindfulness foundations
- emotional awareness
- communication skills
- perspective-shifting abilities
- daily routines
- nervous system regulation
- Zen-aligned habits

This is the framework you will use to interpret every story later.

**PHASE 2 — The 50 Zen Story Practice Template**

Each story has:

- a summary
- an emotional check-in
- an insight reflection
- a Dharma connection
- a guided meditation
- an embodied practice
- a journal prompt
- a Zen affirmation

These transformations lead to deep personal practice, such as attending 50 mini mindfulness sessions on your own.

**What You Will Gain from This Workbook**

By the end of this journey, you will notice yourself thinking more clearly and responding rather than reacting. You will begin to regulate your emotions with greater ease and understand your mind's patterns, rather than feeling controlled by them. Stressful situations will feel less overwhelming, and you will move through them with a calmer, steadier presence. You will speak with more awareness, listen with more depth, and naturally break the anxiety loops that once felt unmanageable. Sleep will improve, relationships will become healthier, and inner peace will feel more accessible. Most importantly, you will begin to take back control of your thoughts and feel more grounded in your true self. You will learn how to cultivate presence, steadiness, compassion, mindfulness, emotional resilience, and a deep connection to your inner life.

**After the Workbook**

When the last story is complete and your final reflection has settled, your journey does not end here. This is where *Yīng Huā Forest* marks its presence—a quiet path to continue your practice. Created from the same heart as these pages, *Yīng Huā Forest* offers a space to live the teachings day by day. At the end of this workbook, you'll find simple next steps—a gentle guide to help you carry the stillness forward.

**My Journey — and Why I Wrote This Workbook**

Every author tells a story, but a mindfulness author gives a reason. This workbook exists because I have seen minds transformed, hearts softened, anxiety dissolved, clarity awakened, and inner strength restored—not because life became easier, but because people finally learned how to meet life with presence. I have witnessed firsthand how mindfulness reshapes emotional resilience, relationship patterns, self-worth, decision-making, stress responses, and long-standing habit cycles. The Zen Forest stories were written to illuminate the inner world, and this workbook was created to help you live the transformation that those stories whisper to you. You are not alone on this path; the forest walks with you.

**A Gentle Call to Continue**

You made the right choice by picking up this workbook.

You've already taken your first step toward calmer days, softer nights, deeper peace, emotional clarity, mindful living, aligned choices, inner strength, and gentle self-compassion.

Now, turn the page. Let's begin this journey with intention, awareness, and a quiet commitment to your own well-being. The forest is waiting for you.

With warmth and gratitude,

*Sati*

# *Before You Begin*

*A Gentle Reminder*

In our eagerness to learn, we often rush past the very moment that prepares us to receive. Before the practices, before the teachings, before the fifty stories that will become your companions—pause here. Take a single breath. Let your mind settle just enough to notice where you are. This small pause is not a delay; it is your first step into mindful awareness.

The *introduction* you just read is more than a beginning—it is the quiet doorway into the work ahead. It explains how this workbook walks beside you, not as a set of instructions, but as a guide into presence, clarity, and emotional steadiness. Zen cannot be absorbed through information alone. It must be lived, sensed, practiced, and gently integrated. Remember to keep a journal at all times alongside this workbook.

*Whispers of the Zen Forest Workbook* is not simply an extension of the stories—it is your practice ground. Your space to explore, to breathe, to reflect, and to become more aware of the patterns within you. Each page is an invitation to slow down, listen inward, and grow with intention.

If you skimmed this section at first, that's alright. Simply return—not out of correction, but out of care for yourself. Let this journey begin not with haste, but with a quiet promise to be present for what unfolds.

# *Phase 1: Foundations*

Welcome, Peace Seeker,

Before you enter the deeper forest of Zen stories, Phase 1 offers you something essential—*a steady foundation.* Think of this section as the quiet clearing before your journey truly begins. When the mind is overwhelmed, it acts like a house with open windows during a storm: thoughts rush in, emotions scatter, and everything feels chaotic. Many people try to force silence or control their thoughts, but Zen invites a gentler approach.

We do not fight the storm; we learn to stand steadily within it.

We do not chase thoughts; we allow them to pass like clouds.

We do not judge our emotions; we learn to understand them.

Phase 1 helps you cultivate exactly that understanding. These nine chapters provide the psychological insight and practical tools necessary to help you recognize your mental patterns, respond rather than react, and create space between stimulus and action.

In this phase, you will learn to:

- Understand how your mind works and why it becomes overwhelmed
- Build a mindfulness foundation that supports emotional stability
- Recognize emotional patterns without getting trapped in them
- Communicate with clarity and less reactivity
- Shift perspectives when you feel stuck or anxious
- Establish daily routines that regulate your nervous system
- Create Zen-aligned habits that ground your inner life

These teachings help you see the stories in *Whispers of the Zen Forest* more clearly—*and* begin to see your own life as a teacher. With this foundation, everyday moments become lessons, and even challenges carry wisdom.

Pause for a breath.

Soften your shoulders.

Let the mind rest.

Perfection isn't needed—only sincerity.

Now step into Phase 1, where clarity begins.

# Chapter 1: The Five Mindfulness Trainings

### *Foundations for Ethical, Emotional, and Mental Well-Being*

**Integrating Ancient Buddhist Ethics with Modern Mindfulness Psychology**

In Buddhism, mindfulness is never practiced alone. It is part of a unified path known as the *Threefold Training*, which consists of:

- *Sīla* — ethical conduct and the Five Mindfulness Trainings
- *Samādhi* — concentration, or a stable and focused mind
- *Prajñā* — insight, or clear understanding of reality

The Buddha taught that these three must grow together. Ethical behavior stabilizes the nervous system and creates inner safety; concentration deepens awareness; and insight transforms understanding. This is why mindfulness is not simply a technique—it is a way of living.

Modern psychology mirrors this structure. Emotional clarity and inner calm only develop when our daily actions do not contradict our values. When behavior, speech, and intentions generate harm, conflict, or guilt, the mind becomes fragmented. But when actions align with compassion, integrity, and awareness, the mind becomes coherent and peaceful.

The *Five Mindfulness Trainings*—known traditionally as the *Pañca-sīla*—offer a practical foundation for a life of clarity. They are also known as the *Five Great, Faultless Gifts* (as mentioned in Anguttara Nikaya 8.39 (AN8.39)*, Tipitaka), because practicing them brings *"freedom from danger, animosity, and oppression"* to countless beings, while granting the same freedom to the practitioner.

The following pages integrate the classical Pāli precepts, modern formulations (from books such as *For a Future to Be Possible by Rev. Thich Nhat Hanh*), and an updated psychological interpretation relevant to contemporary life. The result is a compassionate, grounded, and meaningful path of practice.

### *First: Respect for Life through Compassion*

*"Panatipata veramani sikkhapadam samadiyami."*

*Translated from the original Pāli: I undertake the precept to refrain from destroying living creatures.*

This training begins with *Karuṇā - compassion.* In ancient texts, the instruction was simple: do not kill. But its true meaning expands to:

- Protecting all life
- Acting with non-harm
- Practicing gentleness
- Refusing to support systems of violence
- Caring for sentient and non-sentient beings
- Avoiding harm in thought, speech, and action

Reverence for Life includes not supporting harm indirectly—through choices, consumption, or silence. This expanded understanding is beautifully expressed in a reminder we are meant to carry in our daily awareness:

> *"Aware of the suffering caused by the destruction of life, I am committed to cultivating compassion and learning ways to protect the lives of people, animals, plants, and minerals. I am determined not to kill, not to let others kill, and not to condone any act of killing in the world, in my thinking, and in my way of life."*
>
> *— Thich Nhat Hanh, For a Future to Be Possible*

**Psychological Interpretation**

Harm—through violence, anger, criticism, or even self-neglect—activates the body's threat system. Cortisol rises, breath shortens, and empathy decreases. The nervous system interprets aggression, even inner aggression, as danger.

Compassion, on the other hand, activates circuits that regulate emotions and foster connection. It reduces stress, lowers blood pressure, and increases resilience.

Choosing non-harm is choosing inner calm.

**The First Faultless Gift**

The Buddha said that abandoning killing gives "freedom from danger, animosity, and oppression" to limitless beings—and grants the same freedom to the practitioner (AN 8.39). This precept is the beginning of peace.

### ***Second: True Happiness through Generosity***

*"Adinnadana veramani sikkhapadam samadiyami."*

*Translated from the original Pāli: I undertake the precept to refrain from taking that which is not given.*

This training acknowledges that happiness rooted in taking, grasping, or exploiting can never be stable. Today, "taking what is not given" includes:

- Taking someone's time without respect
- Taking emotional labor without reciprocation
- Taking credit that does not belong to us
- Taking more resources than we need
- Taking joy or peace from others through our actions
- Taking from the Earth without mindfulness

It also includes stealing from **ourselves**—our rest, our dignity, our mental health. This broader interpretation is reflected in a guiding principle we are encouraged to hold close in everyday awareness:

> *"Aware of the suffering caused by exploitation, social injustice, stealing, and oppression, I am committed to cultivating loving kindness and learning ways to work for the well-being of people, animals, plants, and minerals. I will practice generosity by sharing my time, energy, and material resources with those who are in real need. I am determined not to steal and not to possess anything that should belong to others... and to prevent others from profiting from human suffering or the suffering of other species."*
>
> *— Thich Nhat Hanh, For a Future to Be Possible*

**Psychological Interpretation**

Dopamine-driven craving fuels anxiety and dissatisfaction. The more we grasp, the more restless we become. True happiness comes from generosity, sufficiency, and the ability to whisper, "What I have is enough."

**The Second Faultless Gift**

When we refrain from exploitation, we give freedom and safety to countless beings—and participate in that same freedom ourselves (AN 8.39).

This precept teaches us to walk gently on Earth.

### *Third: Love with Responsibility*

*"Kamesu micchacara veramani sikkhapadam samadiyami."*

*Translated from the original Pāli: I undertake the precept to refrain from sexual misconduct.*

Sexual misconduct includes manipulation, coercion, infidelity, using sexuality to escape emotional pain, or violating someone's trust. Real love requires responsibility, clarity, and consent. This enriched perspective is embodied in a teaching meant to stay present in our awareness as we move through the world:

> *"Healthy intimacy is psychologically grounding; harmful intimacy destabilizes the heart. Aware of the suffering caused by sexual misconduct, I am committed to cultivating responsibility and learning ways to protect the safety and integrity of individuals, couples, families, and society. I am determined not to engage in sexual relations without love and a long-term commitment... I will do everything in my power to protect children from sexual abuse and to prevent couples and families from being broken by sexual misconduct."*
>
> *— Thich Nhat Hanh, For a Future to Be Possible*

**Psychological Interpretation**

Sexuality is deeply tied to attachment, self-worth, and emotional safety. Violating this training leads to shame, guilt, and long-term emotional fragmentation. Practicing it creates stability, trust, and deep respect.

**The Third Faultless Gift**

When harmful intimacy is abandoned, beings experience freedom from danger and exploitation—and the practitioner experiences the same (AN 8.39).

This precept protects the heart.

### *Fourth: Loving Speech and Deep Listening through Mindful Communication*

*"Musavada veramani sikkhapadam samadiyami."*

*Translated from the original Pāli: I undertake the precept to refrain from incorrect speech.*

Incorrect speech includes lying, gossip, exaggeration, harshness, criticism, slander, and speaking from anger. Loving speech transforms relationships, protects emotional safety, and cultivates trust.

Deep listening is a healing practice—it allows others to feel seen and heard. This deeper understanding is captured in a gentle reminder meant to accompany us through each moment of daily life:

> *"Aware of the suffering caused by unmindful speech and the inability to listen to others, I am committed to cultivating loving speech and deep listening... Knowing that words can create happiness or suffering, I am determined to speak truthfully, with words that inspire confidence, joy, and hope... I will refrain from words that cause division or discord and will make every effort to reconcile and resolve all conflicts."*
>
> *— Thich Nhat Hanh, For a Future to Be Possible*

**Psychological Interpretation**

Words shape neural pathways. Angry speech activates the fight-or-flight response; gentle speech activates oxytocin and promotes calm. Relationships flourish when communication becomes mindful.

**The Fourth Faultless Gift**

By refraining from harmful speech, we free countless beings from fear, confusion, and hurt—and we, too, share in that freedom (AN 8.39).

This precept protects connection.

### *Fifth: Nourishment and Healing through Mindful Consumption*

*"Suramerayamajja pamadatthana veramani sikkhapadam samadiyami."*

*Translated from the original Pāli: I undertake the precept to refrain from intoxicating drinks and drugs which lead to carelessness.*

Today's intoxicants extend far beyond alcohol. Digital addiction, social media obsession, binge-watching, doom-scrolling, emotional eating, compulsive shopping, pornography, fear-driven news, and toxic conversations all cloud mental clarity.

This understanding is summed up in a daily reminder we are meant to keep close to heart:

*"Aware of the suffering caused by unmindful consumption, I am committed to cultivating good health, both physical and mental... I will ingest only items that preserve peace, well-being, and joy... I am determined not to use alcohol or any intoxicant, or to ingest foods or items that contain toxins, such as certain TV programs, magazines, books, films, and conversations... I understand that a proper diet is crucial for self-transformation and for the transformation of society."*

*— Thich Nhat Hanh, For a Future to Be Possible*

**Psychological Interpretation**

Intoxicants hijack dopamine pathways, reduce impulse control, increase anxiety, and numb emotional awareness. Mindful consumption fosters mental spaciousness, emotional grounding, and clarity, which are essential for deep practice.

**The Fifth Faultless Gift**

When we refrain from intoxicants, we protect countless beings (including ourselves) from carelessness, confusion, and harm—and experience the same protection in return (AN 8.39). This precept protects clarity.

## *Why Ethical Living Leads to Inner Peace*

The Five Mindfulness Trainings, also known as the Five Precepts, reduces inner conflict, stabilizes relationships, and strengthens emotional regulation. When our outer behavior aligns with inner values, mindfulness naturally becomes easier. Ethical living creates a calm mind. A calm mind creates steady concentration. Steady concentration opens the door to deep insight. This is the architecture of transformation.

### *Reflection Before Moving Forward*

Take a moment to reflect:

- Which training resonates most with your life right now?
- Where do you sense tension or conflict in your actions?
- What small change can you make this week to practice these trainings gently and steadily?

# Chapter 2: The Four Noble Truths

### *Understanding Suffering and the Path to Liberation: A Clear, Modern Exploration of the Buddha's Most Foundational Teaching*

If the Five Mindfulness Trainings form the ethical foundation of inner peace, the Four Noble Truths (as mentioned in Samyutta Nikaya 56.11 (SN 56.11)**, Tipitaka) form the psychological map of human suffering—and the pathway out of it. This teaching is often misunderstood by some as a philosophical theory, but it is deeply practical. It explains why the mind struggles, why anxiety arises, why dissatisfaction persists, and how peace becomes possible.

Just as a physician identifies an illness, its cause, its possibility of cure, and the treatment plan, the Buddha offered this structure to diagnose the human condition. Far from pessimistic, it is a compassionate framework for healing—emotionally, mentally, and spiritually.

In modern terms, the Four Noble Truths help us understand:

- Why do we repeat unhelpful patterns?
- Why does anxiety appear even in moments of calm?
- Why the mind clings to stories and fears,
- Why does contentment slip away so quickly?
- How to train the mind toward clarity instead of chaos?

Let us explore each Truth with clarity and compassion.

### *The First Noble Truth — "This is Suffering" (Dukkha)*

**Recognizing the Reality of Inner Struggle**

The Buddha's first insight was unwavering honesty: life, in its ordinary form, contains suffering. Not dramatic suffering alone, but the subtle forms too, which includes:

- the dissatisfaction that lingers even during success
- the fatigue of constant striving
- the ache of impermanence
- the heaviness of emotional expectations
- the anxiety of not knowing what comes next

This truth is not meant to depress—it is meant to *wake us up.* We suffer not because life is flawed, but because we resist its nature.

Modern psychology echoes this: suppressed emotions intensify, avoidance strengthens fear, and denial leads to fragmentation. Recognition, by contrast, softens the heart.

To see suffering clearly is the first moment of freedom.

### *The Second Noble Truth — "This is the Origin of Suffering" (Samudaya)*

**Understanding Craving, Clinging, and Misperception**

Suffering has causes. The Buddha identified three:

- **Craving (tanhā)** — wanting, grasping, chasing
- **Clinging** — holding onto what must naturally change
- **Ignorance** — misperceiving reality, confusing stories for truth

Craving produces tension. Clinging produces fear. Ignorance produces confusion. Together, they create patterns of:

- "If only…"
- "I must have…"
- "This should not be happening…"
- "Why isn't life staying the way I want?"

This Truth is liberating because it shows suffering is not random. It has roots that can be seen, understood, and gradually released.

### *The Third Noble Truth — "This is the Cessation of Suffering" (Nirodha)*

**The Possibility of Inner Peace**

The Buddha's brilliance shines here: If the causes of suffering can be understood, they can be transformed. Cessation does not mean life becomes perfect. It means the *mind stops fighting with life.* Suffering ends when we stop clinging, chasing, or resisting every emotion.

Peace is born when:

- craving softens,
- clinging loosens,
- and clarity replaces confusion.

This is not a mystical disappearance of pain—it is the realization that pain does not need to become suffering, and thus inner liberation is possible.

### *The Fourth Noble Truth — "This is the Path" (Magga)*

**The Noble Eightfold Path as Practice**

The Fourth Truth is the path out of suffering. It is called the *Noble Eightfold Path (SN 56.11)*, a training that transforms behavior, speech, habits, thoughts, and attention.

This path includes:

- **Right View** — seeing reality clearly
- **Right Intention** — acting from kindness, simplicity, and non-harm
- **Right Speech** — truthful, compassionate communication
- **Right Action** — ethical, grounded behavior
- **Right Livelihood** — work that does not harm
- **Right Effort** — cultivating wholesome qualities
- **Right Mindfulness** — awareness of body, feelings, mind, and phenomena
- **Right Concentration** — steady, collected attention

The Path is not a rulebook. It is a *training of the heart and mind,* one small step at a time.

Modern psychology reflects the same elements:

- cognitive clarity,
- emotional regulation,
- nervous system balance,
- values-based behavior,
- mindful communication,
- focus and attention training.

The Noble Eightfold Path is not an ancient theory; it is a living, breathing practice.

### *Why These Truths Matter for Modern Life*

We repeat patterns because we cling to the familiar. We suffer because we resist change. We struggle because we want certainty in a world built on movement. But suffering is not a punishment—it is a signal.

A signal telling us:

- something needs to be seen,
- something needs to be understood,
- something needs to be released.

The Four Noble Truths give us the tools to decode that signal.

They show us that:

- suffering has a cause,
- that cause can be known,
- it can be softened, released, and transformed,
- and there is a step-by-step path guiding us through that transformation.

This teaching is the foundation of all mindful living.

### *From Chapter 46 of the Book "Whispers of the Zen Forest (WOTZF)" to Your Own Life Chapter*

Chapter 46 of *WOTZF* is not merely a story. It is a *map*—a quiet lantern lighting the way through the Buddha's most essential teaching.

The Four Noble Truths illuminate:

- why you suffer,
- how that suffering is maintained,
- why it can end,
- and how this workbook walks with you through the process of letting go.

As you move forward, remember

You are not just filling pages. You are rewiring your mind. You are reshaping your habits. You are reclaiming your inner clarity. You are walking your own Noble Eight-fold Path—*one breath, one insight, one compassionate choice at a time.*

***Reflection Before Moving Forward***

Sit with these questions gently:

- Where in your life do you notice subtle suffering?
- What do you tend to cling to? Control? Identity? Relationships?
- How might softening craving reduce anxiety?
- What would inner freedom look like for you?

Let these reflections settle like leaves drifting softly to the forest floor.

# Chapter 3: Zen Foundations: Letting Go and Returning to Your True Self

### *How Simplicity, Presence, and Non-Grasping Restore Inner Freedom*

Zen is often described as simple, but simplicity is not the absence of depth—it is the stripping away of everything that is not essential. In Zen, the foundational movement is always the same: *letting go.* Not letting go as rejection, suppression, or forced detachment, but letting go as a natural softening—an unclenching of the mind.

The Buddha taught that the nature of the mind is clear, spacious, and aware. What distorts this natural clarity is not life itself but the layers of craving, fear, judgment, resistance, and identity we place on top of experience. Zen calls this overlay "the clouds"—temporary obscurations that cover the sky but never alter the sky itself.

Chapter 3 is an invitation to rediscover that sky within you.

Let us begin with the foundations.

### *Returning to Simplicity*

**The Art of Meeting the Present Moment as It Is**

Zen begins where complications end. Not by making life smaller, but by seeing life without the mental commentary that complicates everything unnecessarily.

Simplicity is not minimalism. It is the ability to meet the moment without adding assumptions, stories, projections, comparisons, fears about the future, and replays of the past.

When simplicity becomes a way of being, the mind stops creating suffering where none is needed. This is why Zen monks speak slowly, move intentionally, and observe the smallest gestures with full attention.

Modern psychology refers to this as *"reducing cognitive load."* Zen calls it *"coming home."* Simplicity is how you return to your original clarity—the clarity beneath noise, beneath hurry, beneath old patterns.

Letting go begins here.

### *The Zen Principle of Non-Grasping*

**Why Holding On Creates Tension — and How Release Creates Peace**

At the heart of Zen lies one essential insight:

*Suffering arises from grasping. Peace arises from release.*

Grasping is not just clinging; it is the mental tightening around expectations:

- wanting situations to remain the same
- wanting emotions to disappear
- wanting people to behave as we wish
- wanting guarantees, stability, or validation
- wanting a future, we can control

Each grasp creates internal tension. Each release creates internal space. Zen does not ask you to abandon desire. Zen asks you to see where desire gives rise to contraction.

Non-grasping is the art of loosening the mind's fist.

When grasping softens, the nervous system shifts from a state of fight-or-flight into one of ease. Breath deepens. Thoughts slow. Awareness widens. You begin to sense a quiet strength underneath the surface of your life.

This is your true self—not the anxious self, not the reactive self, but the spacious self.

### *The Practice of Returning*

**How Zen Guides You Back to the Mind Beneath the Noise**

Zen practice is not about achieving a perfect state of mind. It is about *returning*—again and again—to the place within you that is already still.

The return happens through:

• *Breath*

Each breath is a bridge from mind to body, from story to presence. It represents a link between the external environment and your inner world, encompassing both physical and mental spaces.

• *Awareness*

Noticing sensations, thoughts, or emotions without judgment or resistance.

• *Non-Identification*

Recognizing that you *have* thoughts…but you are not your thoughts. You *experience* emotions…but they do not define you.

• *Openness*

Allowing each moment to be exactly as it is, without tightening around it.

Zen teacher whisper:

*"When distracted, return.*
*When lost, return.*
*When overwhelmed, return."*

The power of Zen is not in never being carried away. The power is in *always coming back*. Returning again and again is how the mind remembers its true shape.

### *Letting Go as a Path Back to Self*

Letting go is not giving up. Letting go is returning. Returning to:

- your breath,
- your awareness,
- your clarity,
- your presence,
- your groundedness.

Zen teaches that your true self is not something you must find. It is something you uncover by removing what is not you:

- fear,
- conditioning,
- defensiveness,
- overthinking,
- inner noise.

When these soften, your deeper nature—calm, compassionate, steady—reveals itself without effort. You do not build the true self. You uncover it.

### *Zen Foundations in Modern Life*

The beauty of Zen is that it does not require escaping your current life. It transforms your relationship **to** your life.

- Washing dishes becomes meditation.
- Drinking tea becomes mindfulness.
- Walking your dog becomes a moment of peace.
- Pausing before speaking becomes compassion.
- Not reacting becomes liberation.
- Returning to awareness becomes strength.

Zen teaches that enlightenment is found not in monasteries alone, but in ordinary moments lived with extraordinary presence. Your life becomes the practice. Your mind becomes the temple. Your breath becomes the teacher.

### *Your True Self Is Always Here*

The true self in Zen is not mystical; it is simple: the part of you that is aware, spacious, grounded, unburdened. It cannot be lost. It can only be forgotten. And remembering is the essence of mindfulness. Letting go is remembering. Returning is remembering. Being present is remembering.

### *Reflection Before Moving Forward*

Take a moment to sit quietly. Breathe gently. Let these questions guide you inward:

1. What are you holding onto that is creating tension? A belief? A fear? A memory? An expectation?
2. Where does your mind tighten the most—relationships, work, identity, or control?
3. When was the last time you felt spacious, open, or grounded? What were you doing?
4. Where can you practice returning—today, in a simple and compassionate way?

Let the answers arise softly. They do not need to be perfect. They only need to be honest.

# Chapter 4: The Inner Architecture That Supports a Clear, Stable Mind

Mindfulness is often mistaken for a technique: *breathe slowly, observe the present moment, stay calm.* But mindfulness is not merely an exercise—it is a *way of being.* It is the capacity to remain awake and aware within our own lives, even when the mind is loud, the emotions are strong, or life is uncertain.

In Zen, mindfulness is described as *the lamp inside the mind*—the light that reveals reality as it is, not as we fear it may be or as we wish it would be.

To cultivate this inner lamp, Zen identifies a set of essential supports known as *the mindfulness pillars.* These pillars strengthen attention, calm the nervous system, clarify perception, and help us live with deeper presence.

This chapter explores these pillars—not as abstract concepts, but as practical foundations that transform daily life.

## *Awareness of the Body*

### The Body as Home, Anchor, and Teacher

The body is the most honest part of our experience. It does not pretend, distort, dramatize, or deny. It responds exactly to what is happening - breath quickens, muscles tense, the stomach tightens, the shoulders lift, the jaw locks. This is why the first pillar of mindfulness is *bodily awareness.*

Zen teaches: *"Return to the body, and the mind will follow."*

Modern neuroscience agrees. Sensory awareness anchors attention, stabilizes emotion, and pulls the mind out of spiraling thought.

When you become aware of:

- your posture,
- your breath,
- the movement of your hands,
- the weight of your feet,
- the sensation of sitting or standing or any other bodily sensation,

something quiet begins to shift. You step out of your head and return to your life. The body becomes a refuge—not a battlefield.

### *Awareness of Feelings and Emotions*

**Learning to Sense Without Being Overwhelmed**

The second mindfulness pillar is learning to recognize emotions without becoming entangled in them. In Buddhism, feelings are classified as:

- pleasant,
- unpleasant,
- or neutral.

That's it. The stories, judgments, and reactions come later. Zen teaches that if you can observe the raw feeling—before the story is added—your relationship with suffering transforms.

For example, sometimes:

- Anger is heat in the chest.
- Fear is tightness in the stomach.
- Sadness is heaviness behind the eyes.
- Peace is warmth in the body.

When you recognize feelings as *sensations* instead of *threats*, you gain freedom. You can breathe with them. You can hold them gently. You can let them move through you instead of letting them define you.

This pillar teaches emotional intelligence at its deepest level.

### *Awareness of Thoughts*

**Seeing the Mind Without Becoming the Mind**

Most suffering does not come from what happens—it comes from the thinking we attach to what happens. Mindfulness allows us to observe thoughts like clouds floating across a wide sky. Some are dark, some are bright, some are noisy, and some are soft. But they all pass.

The third mindfulness pillar is recognizing:

- "This is a thought."
- "This is a story."
- "This is a mental habit."
- "This is not who I am."

Zen masters whisper:

*"Thoughts are guests. You are the host."*

Modern cognitive psychology mirrors this: when you learn to depersonalize thoughts, anxiety loses its grip. This pillar teaches you to respond rather than react, to witness your thoughts instead of getting lost in them.

***Awareness of Habits and Impulses***

**The Hidden Patterns That Shape Your Life**

Every mind develops automatic habits:

- rushing,
- overthinking,
- people-pleasing,
- interrupting,
- reacting quickly,
- reaching for your phone when uncomfortable,
- eating when emotional,
- replaying conversations,
- fixating on what-ifs.

Mindfulness helps you *see* these impulses the moment they arise. When you can see the impulse, you create space. In that space, freedom appears.

Zen teaches: *"To see your habit is to loosen its power."*

This pillar strengthens self-regulation, breaks old patterns, and restores inner choice.

### *Awareness of Reality as It Is*

**The Most Transformative Pillar of All**

The final mindfulness pillar is the ability to see things clearly—without distortion, expectation, or projection. Reality is often simple. It is our mental commentary that complicates it.

Zen calls this pillar *"seeing through the eyes of presence."*

When this pillar is strong, you experience situations as they truly are:

- not as your fears paint them,
- not as your past distorts them,
- not as your impatience rushes them,
- not as your expectations shape them.

You begin to meet life without beliefs, labels, or judgments blocking your view. This clarity is the beginning of wisdom.

### *Bringing the Pillars Into Daily Life*

Mindfulness pillars are not meant for meditation cushions alone. They are meant for:

- brushing your teeth,
- washing dishes,
- speaking with your child,
- replying to a message,
- walking to work,
- sitting in traffic,
- navigating conflict,
- making decisions,
- or simply breathing.

Each moment becomes a practice ground.

When these pillars strengthen, your inner foundation becomes unshakeable. Stress decreases. Reactivity softens. Clarity grows. Presence deepens. You begin to live from your true center.

### *Reflection Before Moving Forward*

Sit quietly for a few breaths. Let the mind settle like dust in sunlight. Reflect gently:

1. Which pillar feels most natural to you right now?
2. Which pillar is the most challenging—and why?
3. Where does your awareness tend to drift: body, emotions, thoughts, habits, or stories?
4. What is one daily activity where you can practice a little more presence today?
5. How would your life feel if you met each moment with just 10% more awareness?

Let these reflections guide your next step. Mindfulness happens one small shift at a time.

# Chapter 5: Guided Practices to Build a Simple, Zen-Based Daily Routine

### *Creating Rhythm, Presence, and Stability Through Gentle Daily Rituals*

Zen practice is never about forcing the mind into silence. It is about creating a life where silence can naturally arise. Where presence can breathe. Where attention can settle. Where the heart can soften without being asked. A Zen routine, therefore, is not rigid or demanding — it is supportive, nourishing, and shaped by kindness.

In traditional Zen monasteries, the rhythm of the day is built on small yet powerful rituals: waking with awareness, walking mindfully to the dining room, bowing to the meditation hall, pausing before speaking, touching objects with intention, and closing the day with gratitude. These rituals are not designed to impress the mind — they are designed to *free* it.

Modern life is different from monastic life, yet the human mind remains the same. It craves rhythm. It seeks grounding. It relaxes into familiarity. A routine that honors these truths helps the nervous system shift from reactivity into steadiness.

In this chapter, we craft a simple daily rhythm based on Zen wisdom — a rhythm that fits your life, not the other way around. Think of these practices as *beads on a mala:* each one small, complete, and sacred; together, forming a whole.

### *The Zen Morning: Beginning in Stillness Instead of Momentum*

**Awakening the Inner World Before the Outer World Arrives**

The mind wakes before the body. It begins planning, remembering, anticipating, worrying. Zen teaches us to *enter the day before the mind enters us* — to greet the morning with clarity rather than chaos.

A Zen morning has three aims:

- to land in your body
- to calm the mind before it accelerates

- to choose the emotional tone of your day

Let us explore these in depth.

**The First Moment of Awareness**

When the eyes open, there is a small, sacred doorway — a moment when the mind has not yet collected its burdens. Before thoughts rush in, place a hand gently on your chest or belly.

Feel:

- your breath rising and falling,
- the warmth beneath your palm,
- the soft weight of your body,
- the tenderness of simply being alive.

This one gesture communicates to your nervous system:

*"I am here. I am safe. I can begin slowly."*

It is a type of re-parenting — an act of emotional refuge.

**The First Breath of the Day**

In Zen, monks often take one deliberate breath before rising. Not deep, not dramatic — simply honest. A breath that whispers:

*"I am entering this day with awareness."*

One breath to arrive. One breath to clear the fog. One breath to reclaim your morning from autopilot.

This becomes the anchor that steadies you long before emails, messages, or responsibilities appear. Focus on your breathing for at least 1-2 minutes before standing up

**Setting an Intention of Being, Not Doing**

Before your feet touch the floor, ask:

*"How do I want my inner world to feel today?"*

Not how productive you want to be, but how you want to *be:*

- Calm?
- Grounded?
- Compassionate?
- Patient?

- Steady?
- Soft?

Your emotional intention becomes the lens through which you move. It shapes your reactions, your speech, your decisions. Intention is the quiet architecture of every mindful day.

***The Zen Day: Weaving Awareness into Ordinary Moments***

**The World Does Not Need to Change for You to Be Present — Only Your Attention Does**

Your day may be full of meetings, deadlines, caretaking, travel, and responsibilities. Zen does not ask you to reduce your life; it teaches you how to bring stillness *into* your life. The practices that follow are designed to blend naturally into your day, transforming the ordinary into sacred ground.

**The Power of Transitions**

Most stress arises *between* activities, not during them. The mind rushes to what"s next before the body has completed what's now.

Zen teaches us to honor transitions — the sacred spaces between moments.

Before shifting tasks, pause for:

- one conscious breath
- one slow inhale and exhale
- one soft release of the shoulders

This pause fosters psychological spaciousness and helps prevent overwhelm from building up. Keep practicing for a few minutes every time you switch tasks until it becomes a habit. A transition breath is a reset. A return. A promise to stay anchored.

**The Sensory Check-In**

Throughout the day, gently ask:

*"What is my body sensing right now?"*

This question draws the mind out of mental noise and into direct experience.

It might be:

- the sensation of your feet touching the ground
- the temperature of your hands
- the rise and fall of your breath
- the feeling of air on your face
- the sound of distant movement

This is mindfulness in its purest form — attention placed in the present through the body. Every sensory moment is a doorway out of anxiety.

**The Zen Minute: A Pause That Rewires the Nervous System**

Once or twice a day, give yourself one full minute:

- Unclench your jaw
- Drop your shoulders
- Inhale deeply and exhale slowly
- Allow your mind to widen and soften

Neuroscience reveals that a minute of mindful breathing can shift the brain from a state of survival to one of regulation.

In Zen temples, practitioners pause throughout the day — not to escape life, but to return to it. A Zen Minute is enough to change the emotional direction of an entire afternoon.

### *The Zen Evening: Releasing the Day Before Resting the Mind*

**Letting Go of Mental Residue, Softening into Quiet, Inviting Inner Peace**

Evening is when the mind becomes reflective and vulnerable. Memories replay. Conversations echo. Worries multiply. Zen evenings focus on *dissolving the accumulated weight of the day,* so the mind does not carry it into sleep.

**Creating a Soft Ending Ritual**

Choose one symbolic action that signals closure:

- dimming a lamp
- lighting a candle
- brewing warm tea
- closing your laptop
- opening a window

- sitting quietly with your hands resting gently

This ritual tells your mind:

*"The day is complete. I can let go."*

Ritual regulates the nervous system and helps the mind shift from doing to being.

**Evening Reflection Without Judgment**

Zen reflection is not about evaluating performance — it is about understanding experience.

Ask:

- "What nourished me today?"
- "Where did I struggle?"
- "What can I release so it does not follow me into sleep?"

This reflection turns your day into a teacher rather than a burden.

**Preparing the Mind for Rest**

Before sleep, rest your attention on your breath or the sensations in your body.

If thoughts arise, allow them.

If emotions surface, soften around them.

If the mind wanders, return gently.

This is not effort — it is surrender.

In Zen, rest is not the absence of thought; it is the absence of resistance to thought.

A peaceful night begins with a softened heart.

## *Living Your Day as a Zen Practitioner*

A Zen day is never perfect — it is *intentional.*

Zen is composed of small returns, gentle pauses, quiet breaths, simple rituals, awareness in everyday moments, and self-directed compassion.

Over time, clarity deepens, reactivity softens, patience expands, emotional resilience strengthens, presence becomes effortless, and the inner world grows calmer, quieter, and lighter.

This is how Zen enters your life — not through dramatic change, but through *slow, steady reorientation toward presence.*

### *Reflection Before Moving Forward*

Return to your breath. Let the mind settle like water in a clear bowl.

Reflect deeply:

1. Which part of your day tends to pull you away from presence — mornings, afternoons, or evenings? Why?
2. What would it feel like to begin your day with one intentional breath?
3. Which small Zen anchor — a transition breath, a sensory check-in, a closing ritual — feels most natural to you?
4. Where does your mind tighten the most? Can you soften there, even a little? If yes, then how?
5. If your daily life became 1% more mindful, what might shift in your emotional world?

Let your reflections stay gentle. Nothing must be fixed. Everything begins with awareness.

# Chapter 6: Reflection Prompts to Slow Down and Shift Inner Perspective

### *Questions That Open the Heart and Reveal the Landscape Within*

Reflection in Zen is not analysis. It is neither mental effort nor self-critique. Reflection is *seeing* — seeing yourself clearly, without judgment, without distortion, without rushing to fix or improve. It is like holding a lantern toward your inner world and noticing what has been alive in you.

These prompts are not meant to be answered quickly. They are meant to *slow your breath, quiet the mind, and help you uncover truths beneath the surface.* Each prompt is an invitation; each answer is a beginning.

Use these reflections as:

- daily check-ins,
- journaling practices,
- meditation companions,
- or moments of inner honesty during the day.

Let these prompts soften your inner world with compassion.

### *Seeing Yourself Clearly*

**Understanding the Landscape of Your Mind and Emotions**

Before transformation comes understanding. Zen teaches that what you can see, you can release. What remains unseen continues to silently control your inner life.

These reflections help you notice:

- where your mind tightens,
- where emotions gather,
- where tenderness is needed,
- and where clarity is waiting.

**Reflection Prompts**

- Where do I feel the most resistance in my life right now — and what emotion lies beneath it?
- What am I afraid to feel, and why?
- If my body could speak, what would it tell me about how I've been living?
- What thoughts keep returning, and what do they want me to understand?
- What am I holding onto that is quietly exhausting me?

These questions reveal the emotional knots beneath the surface of the mind.

### *Softening the Inner Critic*

**Letting Go of Harshness, Comparison, and Pressure**

Many people carry an inner critic — a voice that judges, compares, demands, pushes, and punishes. Zen reminds us gently: *"You do not grow by beating the mind. You grow by understanding it."*

The following reflections help loosen the grip of inner harshness.

**Reflection Prompts**

- Where in my life am I the hardest on myself, and what am I trying to protect?
- How would my decisions change if I treated myself with the kindness I offer others?
- What expectations of myself feel heavy, unrealistic, or inherited — not chosen?
- If I could speak to myself as a wise friend, what would I say today?
- What am I ready to forgive myself for?

These questions dissolve self-judgment and make space for self-compassion.

### *Releasing the Past, Meeting the Present*

**Healing Through Presence Rather Than Repetition**

The mind often lives in reruns — replaying past pain, past conversations, past mistakes. Zen teaches that healing begins when the past is *acknowledged* but not allowed to occupy the present.

These reflections help reveal what still needs space, care, or release.

**Reflection Prompts**

- What am I still carrying from the past that no longer belongs to me?
- Which memories still shape my reactions today?
- What apology do I owe myself?
- If today were a new beginning, what would I choose to leave behind?
- What part of me is still waiting to be acknowledged?

Reflection becomes liberation when the past loosens its grip.

## *Understanding Desire, Clinging, and Craving*

### Seeing the Forces That Shape Our Choices

Desire is not wrong. Clinging is where suffering begins. Zen teaches us to see desire clearly — to understand what we seek, why we seek it, and whether it nourishes or empties us.

**Reflection Prompts**

- What am I chasing, and what feeling do I hope it will give me?
- Where do I cling the most — relationships, outcomes, identity, approval?
- What craving creates the most tension in my life?
- If I loosened my grip by just 5%, what might shift?
- What would life feel like if I trusted it a little more?

These prompts help soften grasping and create inner spaciousness.

## *Cultivating Compassion and Interbeing*

### Seeing Yourself and Others With Softer Eyes

Compassion is not sentimental. It is the ability to meet suffering — yours and others' — with warmth instead of fear. When compassion grows, your inner world becomes kinder, relationships become lighter, and the boundaries between self and other begin to soften.

**Reflection Prompts**

- Where does my heart naturally soften, and where does it harden?
- What suffering in others do I understand most deeply — and why?
- Where can I offer compassion today without expecting anything in return?
- What would it look like to treat myself as someone worthy of gentleness?
- Who in my life needs my presence rather than my solutions?

These reflections help you touch the quality of *interbeing* — the understanding that we rise and fall together.

## *Rediscovering Your True Self*

**Uncovering the Quiet, Steady Being Beneath Thoughts**

Your true self is not the anxious voice, not the overthinking mind, not the fear or the doubt. Zen teaches that your true self is the awareness that sees all these things — the part of you that has never been harmed, never been broken, never been lost.

These reflections help you reconnect with that inner spaciousness.

**Reflection Prompts**

- Who am I beneath my roles, achievements, and expectations?
- What moments make me feel most connected to something larger than myself?
- Which qualities in me feel timeless?
- What do I know about myself that fear keeps me from trusting?
- If I lived from my truest self today, what would change?

These questions help peel back layers until the quiet truth inside is visible again.

## *Reflection Before Moving Forward*

Take a slow, grounding breath. Let your shoulders release. Let your face soften. Let the questions settle like petals on water.

Reflect gently:

1. Which reflection prompt spoke to the part of you that is ready to grow?
2. Which question awakened a feeling you have not touched in a while?
3. What truth surfaced that surprised you?
4. Where is your next step — in letting go, softening, or opening?

5. How can you bring today's insight into tomorrow's breath?

There is no right answer. Only honest seeing. Every reflection is a doorway inward.

# Chapter 7: Exercises for Gratitude, Compassion, and Simplicity

### *Training the Heart to See What Is Good, Soft, and Enough*

If mindfulness is the lamp of awareness, then gratitude, compassion, and simplicity are the qualities of light it spreads. They are not just feelings; they are *trainings of the heart.* You don't wait to feel grateful, compassionate, or simple. You *practice* them — gently, consistently — until they become your natural way of being.

Gratitude teaches the mind to notice blessings instead of deficits. Compassion teaches the heart to stay open in the presence of suffering. Simplicity teaches the whole being to rest in "enough".

These three qualities, when combined, create an inner environment where anxiety softens, craving loosens, and peace becomes more accessible. In Zen, they are not side practices; they are central to how we walk, speak, breathe, and relate.

This chapter offers *practical exercises* to cultivate each of these qualities in your everyday life — not as abstract virtues, but as lived experiences.

### *Gratitude — Training the Mind to See What Is Already Here*

Gratitude is not denial; it does not pretend everything is perfect. Instead, it brings balance by helping you see that even in difficulty, something is still supporting you: breath, body, shelter, kindness, a lesson, a chance to begin again.

Psychologically, gratitude rewires the brain to focus on what is present, rather than what is missing. It reduces stress, strengthens resilience, and increases emotional warmth. In Zen terms, gratitude is a bow to reality—a quiet "thank you" to life for its continued existence.

**Exercise 1: The Soft-Edge Gratitude Journal**

Instead of a long list, keep this simple and kind. Each evening, write down just *three things* you are grateful for, but with a twist: add a *feeling* to each one.

For example:

- "I am grateful for my morning tea — it made me feel calm."

- "I am grateful for the message from a friend — it made me feel seen."
- "I am grateful for my body — it carried me through another day."

This transforms gratitude from a mental list into an emotional experience. You are not just naming things; you are reconnecting with how they touched you. Over time, the mind becomes more fluent in noticing small blessings.

**Exercise 2: Gratitude in Difficult Moments**

Choose one challenge in your day — a delay, a conflict, a mistake, a moment of stress. When it happens, do not force positivity. Instead, ask:

- "Is there anything at all I can be grateful for *around* this?"

It might be:

- the lesson you're learning,
- the strength you're building,
- the person who supported you,
- the fact that you are still here, breathing, able to respond.

This practice doesn't eliminate pain; it merely prevents pain from becoming the sole perception in your mind.

**Exercise 3: Gratitude Toward Your Own Effort**

Once a week, sit quietly and ask:

- "What did I carry this week that no one noticed?"
- "Where did I keep going, even when it was hard?"

Then whisper to yourself:

*"Thank you for trying. Thank you for staying. Thank you for showing up."*

You are directing gratitude toward yourself — not as ego, but as acknowledgment. This heals the part of you that feels unseen.

### *Compassion — Meeting Suffering With Warmth Instead of Fear*

Compassion is the ability to stay present with suffering — your own and others' — without turning away, shutting down, or attacking. It is not pity, not fixing, not rescuing. It is the quiet courage to reflect:

*"This is hard. May there be relief. May there be understanding. May there be healing."*
Compassion softens the nervous system, reduces self-criticism, and deepens connection. It is one of the most powerful antidotes to inner harshness.

**Exercise 4: Self-Compassion Break**

When you feel overwhelmed, ashamed, anxious, or exhausted, pause and place a hand over your heart or on your cheek — anywhere that feels comforting.

Then silently whisper three things:

1. *Acknowledgment:* "This is a painful moment."
2. *Common Humanity:* "I am not the only one who feels this way. Others struggle too."
3. *Compassionate Wish:* "May I be kind to myself in this moment."

Even if the mind resists, stay with the gesture. Let the body feel comfort. The words are seeds; the tone is the water.

**Exercise 5: Compassionate Listening (Without Fixing)**

Choose one conversation this week where you decide in advance: *"I will listen more than I speak."*

As the person shares, resist the urge to:

- fix,
- correct,
- advise,
- or change their feelings.

Instead, offer:

- "I hear you."
- "That sounds really hard."
- "Thank you for trusting me with this."

Notice how it feels in your body to hold space simply. This is compassion in relational form.

**Exercise 6: Sending Compassion Quietly**

When you encounter someone struggling — a stranger on the street, a colleague under pressure, a family member in pain — pause inwardly and send a silent phrase:

- “May you find ease.”
- “May you feel supported.”
- “May your suffering lessen.”

You are not trying to control their life. You are training your heart not to harden. This keeps your compassion awake, even when you cannot act outwardly.

### *Simplicity — Discovering That “Enough” Is a Sacred Space*

Simplicity is not deprivation. It is clarity. It is the freedom of not needing everything to be more, better, faster, or different in order to feel at peace. In Zen, simplicity means removing what is unnecessary so that what is essential can be truly seen.

Psychologically, simplicity reduces overstimulation, decision fatigue, comparison, and the anxiety that comes with constant striving.

It does not mean owning less only; it means *wanting less.*

**Exercise 7: The One-Thing Moment**

Once a day, choose *one activity* to do with full attention and without multitasking:

- drinking tea,
- brushing your teeth,
- washing a cup,
- walking from one room to another,
- feeding your pet,
- folding clothes.

During this one activity:

- slow down,
- feel every movement,
- notice sensations,
- stay with what you are doing.

This is simplicity in action: *one moment, one activity, one awareness.* It is the opposite of fragmentation. It is the beginning of inner unity.

**Exercise 8: A Small Letting Go**

Once a week, choose one small thing to simplify:

- one item to give away,
- one digital notification to disable,
- one commitment to gently decline,
- one shelf, drawer, or desktop to clear,
- one expectation of yourself that you consciously soften.

As you let go, whisper quietly:

*"I am creating space for what truly matters."*

Simplicity is not just outer decluttering; it is inner mercy.

**Exercise 9: A Day of Gentle "No"**

Pick one day — or even half a day — to practice the art of **gentle boundary setting**.

When you feel the impulse to say "yes" automatically, pause and ask:

- "Do I genuinely have the capacity for this?"
- "Is this aligned with what I need right now?"

If the answer is no, respond kindly:

- "I would love to, but I don't have the space for it right now."
- "Thank you for thinking of me; I need to rest instead."

This is simplicity in emotional form: not overloading yourself. You are choosing depth over scattering.

### *Gratitude, Compassion, Simplicity — A Single Movement of the Heart*

Though they seem like three separate qualities, gratitude, compassion, and simplicity are deeply connected. When you practice gratitude, you begin to see what is already here. When you practice compassion, you begin to soften toward what is difficult. When you practice simplicity, you begin to stop chasing what is unnecessary.

Together, they whisper:

*"This moment is enough. You are enough. And inside this 'enoughness,' peace can grow."*

These exercises are not requirements. They are *offers* — gentle ways to reclaim your inner world from confusion, noise, and speed.

### *Reflection Before Moving Forward*

Take a moment to sit comfortably. Let your breath move at its own pace. Let your shoulders ease away from your ears. Let your face soften.

Reflect on the following:

1. Which of the three — gratitude, compassion, or simplicity — feels most alive in you right now?
2. Which one feels furthest away, and why do you think that is?
3. Which exercise in this chapter called to you the most — and what does that reveal about what your heart needs?
4. If you practiced just one of these exercises every day for a week, how might your inner world begin to shift?
5. What are you ready to thank, what are you ready to soften toward, and what are you ready to release?

There is no pressure to do everything. Choose one exercise. Begin gently. Let transformation happen quietly, like moss growing in a forest.

# Chapter 8: Meditations, Affirmations, and Breathwork to Ground and Soothe

### *Practices That Bring You Back to Your Center Again and Again*

*Meditation* is not an escape. It is not quieting the mind by force. It is a homecoming — a return to the place inside you that has always been calm, steady, and aware.

*Affirmations* are not forced positivity. They are gentle realignments of the mind, pointing it toward truth instead of fear.

Breathwork, as referred to in this workbook, is not a technique. It is the oldest bridge between body and mind — a direct doorway into peace.

Together, these three practices form a powerful triad that helps you:

- regulate emotions,
- soften anxiety,
- loosen mental rumination,
- quiet inner conflict,
- restore presence,
- and reconnect with your deepest self.

Zen does not separate these practices; it sees them as different expressions of the same intention: *to wake up from the fog of reactive living and return to the clarity of being.*

### *Meditations to Anchor and Steady the Mind*

**Quiet Practices That Bring You Back to Yourself**

Meditation is often misunderstood as a state of sitting with an empty mind. But Zen teaches something far simpler and more compassionate:

*"Meditation is the art of returning."*

Returning to breath. Returning to awareness. Returning to the present moment.

Below are three meditations designed for both beginners and experienced practitioners.

**The "Breath Like a Friend" Meditation**

This meditation teaches you to meet your breath gently — not as a tool, but as a companion.

*How to Practice*

1. Sit with stability and ease: Sit comfortably on a cushion or chair. Keep your spine upright but not rigid, allowing the body to be relaxed and alert.
2. Rest your hands naturally: Place your hands on your lap gently.
3. Bring gentle attention to your natural breath: Close your eyes softly. Feel the natural flow of the breath — *air entering, air leaving.*
4. Inhale through the nose: Let the breath enter naturally, without force. Feel the coolness at the nostrils.
5. Exhale through the nose: Release the breath with gentle ease. Allow the exhalation to soften the body and mind.
6. Add a Quiet Mental Note: With every breath, observe the sense of relaxation flowing through your body.
7. Allow Breath Awareness to Deepen: Stay with the sensations of the breath — the movement, the texture, the rhythm.
8. Return Gently When the Mind Wanders: If thoughts arise, notice them softly. Then guide attention back to the next inhale… and the next exhale.
9. End With One Deep Breath: When the meditation feels complete, take one slow, full breath. Offer yourself a silent moment of gratitude for being present.

Let each breath be a reminder that the body is not your enemy; it is your refuge.

This meditation is especially helpful for:

- anxiety
- restlessness
- emotional overwhelm
- returning to the present after a stressful moment

**The "Noticing Without Fixing" Meditation**

Zen teaches that awareness itself is healing. You don't have to fix what you see — just seeing clearly loosens its grip.

*How to practice:*

1. **Sit in Stillness**: Sit with the body upright and relaxed. Allow the breath to move naturally. Establish the intention to remain aware.
2. **Observe the Arising of Thoughts**: Let the mind settle without trying to control it. When a thought arises, notice it clearly — just as you would notice a sound or a sensation.
3. **Acknowledge Each Thought with a Simple Mental Note**: Remember, *"When there is a mind with thinking, he knows, 'There is a mind with thinking.'"*

Acknowledge softly, according to what appears:

- "thinking,"
- "remembering,"
- "judging,"
- "anticipating,"
- "planning,"
- "fearing,"
- "imagining,"
- "wanting,"
- "resisting,"

Use the simplest, truest label to acknowledge.

4. **Do Not Judge or Follow the Thought**: Do not continue the story. Do not push it away. Do not add emotion to it. Simply recognize: *"This is a thought."*
5. **Let the Thought Pass on Its Own**: As soon as it is noted, allow the thought to dissolve naturally. Do not hold it or react to it. Let it fade the way a wave returns to the sea.
6. **Return to Pure Awareness**: Bring the mind back to the present moment — to the body, to the breath, to the stillness within.
7. **Repeat Without Expectation**: With each new thought, acknowledge and release. Slowly, the mind becomes clearer. Thoughts lose their weight. Awareness becomes steady and spacious.

*Essence of the Practice*

No judgment. No resistance. No lamentation. No story. Only observation. This is insight: seeing thoughts as impermanent events, arising and passing, not-self, empty of solidity.

This is *insight meditation* in everyday language.

This practice reduces:

- rumination,
- catastrophizing,
- emotional spirals,
- cognitive overload.

You begin to see that thoughts do not need your participation to pass.

**The "Body as Ground" Meditation**

When the mind is busy, the body becomes the gateway into stillness.

*How to practice:*

1. Stand naturally and upright: Stand with your feet hip-width apart. Let your knees be soft, not locked. Allow the spine to rise naturally, the body balanced and at ease.
2. Establish awareness of posture: Feel the whole body standing: the weight through the feet, the alignment of the legs, the gentle rise of the torso, the presence of the arms and hands.
3. Bring mindful attention through the body: Slowly sweep your awareness through major areas:
    - the soles of your feet touching the ground,
    - the steadiness of your legs,
    - the natural position of your hands,
    - the openness or tension in your shoulders,
    - the softness of your jaw.

    Notice sensations as they are—warmth, pressure, vibration, heaviness, or ease.

4. Feel the support beneath you: Bring your attention back down to your feet. Sense the firmness, stability, and grounding beneath you. Notice how the earth holds your entire weight without effort.
5. Observe without controlling: Allow sensations to arise and pass through without interfering. Notice subtle swaying, shifting weight, and changes in pressure. Stand with awareness of impermanence — everything moving, changing, alive.
6. Close with a conscious breath: Before ending, take one slow, steady breath. Feel your whole standing posture in this moment. Offer gratitude for the body that carries you.

This practice is especially grounding during:

- panic,
- stress,
- overthinking,
- emotional activation.

It reconnects you to the stability of your physical presence.

## *Affirmations to Reorient the Mind*

### Gentle Words That Point You Toward Truth Instead of Fear

Affirmations in Zen are not about forcing the mind to believe something positive or repeating them to create something; instead, they are about cultivating a state of mind that is open to possibility. They serve to remind the mind of what is already true beneath fear, conditioning, and self-doubt. They aren't used as tools to manifest materialistic things.

Effective affirmations are:

- slow,
- believable,
- compassionate,
- grounded in reality,
- emotionally soothing.

Below are three sets of affirmations designed to calm the mind and open the heart.

**Affirmations for Inner Calm**

Gently whisper when necessary, focusing on your breath during tasks, such as whispering kindness into your own awareness:

- "I can slow down."
- "My breath supports me."
- "I am allowed to rest."
- "I soften my expectations."
- "This moment is enough."

Each affirmation becomes a small invitation back into the present.

**Affirmations for Self-Compassion**

These words serve as a reminder that your value is not based on perfection. Remember to whisper them to yourself during overwhelming times:

- "I am learning. I am growing."
- "My struggles do not define me."
- "I am doing the best I can with what I have."
- "I deserve gentleness."
- "I belong here."

Let the affirmations wrap around the parts of you that feel unseen or overwhelmed.

**Affirmations for Emotional Strength**

These are for moments where doubt rises like a wave:

- "I can face this moment."
- "I have survived every difficult day so far."
- "I trust myself to navigate uncertainty."
- "My inner strength is bigger than my fear."
- "I return to my center again and again."

These affirmations help you stay rooted when the mind becomes chaotic.

*Breathwork to Reset the Nervous System*

**Breathing Patterns That Calm, Clear, and Restore Balance**

Your breath is the only part of your autonomic nervous system you can consciously influence.

It is the switch between:

- anxiety and ease,
- tension and release,
- confusion and clarity.

Below are three grounding breathwork practices that are simple, safe, and deeply soothing. These breathworks are only recommended during extreme stress or anxiety. Otherwise, the *"Breath Like a Friend"* meditation is always the preferred and suggested option.

**The 4–6 Soothing Breath**

This breath reduces anxiety by extending the exhale.

*How to practice:*

- Inhale for 4 seconds,
- Exhale for 6 seconds.

Do this for 1–2 minutes.

The extended exhale signals to the brain: *"I am safe."*

**The Hand-on-Heart Breath**

This breath comforts the emotional body.

*How to practice:*

- Place one hand on your heart.
- Inhale slowly through the nose.
- Exhale softly through the mouth.

As you breathe, focus on the sensations of warmth or cold flowing from your hand into your chest.

This breath is especially helpful for:

- sadness,

- loneliness,
- emotional overwhelm,
- self-criticism.

**The 5–5–5 Breath (Zen Reset Breath)**

This breathwork recenters you when your energy feels scattered or fragmented, and it becomes too difficult to concentrate on your natural breath.

*How to practice:*

- Inhale for 5 seconds,
- Hold for 5 seconds,
- Exhale for 5 seconds.

Repeat softly. If holding for 5 seconds initially feels hard, begin with 3-3-3.

This breath creates clarity and inner steadiness.

### *Meditation, Affirmation, Breath — A Single Path*

These three practices are not separate. They work together:

- Meditation clears the fog.
- Affirmations shift the mind's direction.
- Breathwork calms the nervous system, allowing insight to take hold.

Together, they guide you toward a grounded, soothed, and empowered way of being.

Your breath becomes your anchor. Your awareness becomes your home. Your inner voice becomes your ally.

This is Zen embodied.

In *Whispers of the Zen Forest*, every part of the book gently closes with a meditation, a quiet practice seeded within the book itself. These meditations were written to help you experience the teachings, not just read about them. As you explore the quick grounding practices in this chapter, feel free to return to those meditations as well.

They deepen your understanding. They harmonize with these shorter exercises. They help you build a layered practice — one quick enough for daily use, and one deep enough to reshape your inner world. You may choose one from that book on days when you seek depth, and another from this workbook on days when you need speed and support.

Both paths lead you back to presence. Both are part of your Zen journey.

### ***Reflection Before Moving Forward***

Take a slow, soft breath. Let your eyes relax. Let your shoulders melt. Feel your body supported beneath you.

Reflect on these:

1. Which practice — meditation, affirmation, or breathwork — feels most natural to you?
2. Which one feels new, unfamiliar, or uncomfortable — and what might that reveal?
3. What do you notice in your body when you take a slow, intentional breath?
4. Which affirmation touched the part of you that feels tender or tired?
5. How would your life change if you practiced just one of these exercises every day?

Let your reflection be soft. Let your answers rise on their own. The path unfolds one breath at a time.

# Chapter 9: The Zen Story Deep Practice Template

### *Transforming Every Zen Forest Story Into a Path of Insight, Reflection, and Daily Awakening*

Every story in *Whispers of the Zen Forest* carries a teaching — sometimes soft, sometimes sharp, always revealing. But a Zen story becomes transformative only when it is *entered,* not merely understood. When it becomes a mirror for your mind, a lamp for your awareness, and a bridge between insight and daily life.

This chapter introduces the *Zen Story Deep Practice Template,* the structure you will use for every one of the 50 stories in the workbook. It is designed to guide you gently through the inner landscape the story reveals. This is not a worksheet — it is a *practice rhythm.*

A one-page journey that takes you:

- from story → to understanding
- from understanding → to reflection
- from reflection → to practice
- from practice → to transformation

This is how the forest begins to grow inside you.

### *Why a Deep Practice Template?*

**Because transformation requires structure, rhythm, and intimacy**

Zen does not rely on accumulation — it relies on depth. To deepen awareness, the mind needs a consistent format, a familiar path it can settle into.

A template gives you:

- a gentle rhythm,
- a place to land,
- a ritual to follow,
- and a predictable journey that becomes emotionally safe.

Every time you meet a story, you walk the same inner path — but the insight, the shift, the awakening will be different each time. This repetition builds wisdom. This rhythm creates change. This structure becomes meditation.

### *The Eight-Part Zen Story Deep Practice Template*

**A one-page journey from narrative to awakening**

Each story practice page flows through eight stages:

1. **Story Essence — Entering the Meaning**

   Here you capture the heart of the story in just a few lines. Not a summary — a resonance. What touched you? What image stayed behind? What emotional shift did you feel? This section opens the doorway inward.

2. **Zen Foundation — The Root Principle**

   Every story expresses a core Zen truth:

   - letting go
   - impermanence
   - non-self
   - compassion
   - presence
   - beginner's mind
   - stillness
   - simplicity
   - mindful action
   - wise understanding

   Identifying the principle anchors the story in timeless wisdom.

3. **Teaching Rooted in the Pali Canon**

   Each Zen story echoes the ancient teachings. Here you connect the story to a simple, practical expression of Dhamma:

   "According to the Pali Canon, the Buddha taught ________, and this story reflects that truth by ________."

   This step grounds modern storytelling in ancient insight.

4. **Mindfulness in Practice — Doing, Not Just Knowing**

   A story becomes transformative only when you live it. Each page includes a small practice (2–10 minutes):

   - breathwork
   - grounding
   - letting-go ritual
   - mindful pause
   - compassion gesture
   - silence practice
   - body awareness

   This turns insight into embodiment.

5. **Reflection Prompts — Seeing Yourself in the Story**

   You explore what the story reveals about your patterns:

   - What habit does this story shine a light on?
   - Where do you cling?
   - What fear does it uncover?
   - What truth does it whisper?

   These reflections open the mind to deeper self-awareness.

6. **Gratitude / Compassion / Simplicity Exercise**

   A quick, heart-opening practice aligned with the story:

   - forgiving yourself
   - thanking something quiet
   - releasing a small burden
   - simplifying one expectation
   - offering one silent kindness

   This is the emotional grounding of the page.

7. **Mini-Meditation**

The teaching is sealed not by thinking, but by breathing or meditating. Any 1 simple technique for 1–2 minutes brings the teaching into the body. This moment of presence anchors the insight.

8. **Daily Affirmation — A Seed for the Day**

   One clear sentence to carry with you:

   - "I let go with grace."
   - "My presence is enough."
   - "I return to the light within."

   A small seed of Dhamma that blooms throughout the day as you remember it in your heart, time and again, in between your tasks.

### *How to Use This Template Deeply*

**A short guide for bringing each story to life**

Do not approach each page as a task. Approach it as a meditation.

- *Move slowly.* Take time with each question. Let the story breathe inside you.
- *Write intuitively.* Honesty over perfection. Softness over cleverness.
- *Choose a practice that feels possible.* Small shifts done daily are more transformative than big shifts attempted once.
- *Revisit the page later.* Insights will deepen as the story continues to echo through your day.
- *Let the last line guide your day.* The affirmation is meant to be carried — like a mantra, a thread of awareness.

Remember: This template is not a form. It is a path.

### *The Master Zen Story Workbook Template*

**A One-Page Deep Practice Format for All 50 Stories**

**1. Story Essence**

*A gentle 3–4-line summary capturing the heart of the story — the emotional lesson, the inner movement, and the quiet invitation.*

*Contemplate:*

**2. Zen Foundation**

*Which root Zen principle is awakened by this story?*

Choose the Zen principle the story reflects—whether it points to letting go, impermanence, non-self, compassion, presence, beginner's mind, stillness, simplicity, mindful action, or wise understanding.

*Contemplate:*

**3. Teaching Rooted in the Pali Canon**

*A short paragraph linking the story to the Buddha's teachings in clear, simple language.*

Example structure:

"According to the Pali Canon, the Buddha described __________. This story reflects that truth by showing how __________."

*Contemplate:*

**4. Mindfulness in Practice**

*A small, doable (2–10 minute) practice inspired by the story's message.*

This can be a simple practice such as a breath pattern, a sensory grounding, a mindful pause, a letting-go ritual, a compassionate gesture, a moment of silence, or a gentle noticing exercise.

*Contemplate:*

**5. Reflection Prompts**

*3–5 awareness questions that guide the reader inward.*

*Contemplate:*

**6. Gratitude / Compassion / Simplicity Exercise**

*A quick practice (1–3 minutes) aligned with the story's essence.*

Examples include forgiving yourself for one thing, thanking something quiet that supports you, letting go of a small expectation, offering a silent act of kindness, or releasing a single mental weight.

*Contemplate:*

**7. Mini-Meditation (1–2 Minutes)**

*A simple grounding practice with no jargon.*

Example:

- "Inhale 'soften,' exhale 'release.'"
- 4–6 calming breath
- Hand-on-lap

*Contemplate:*

**8. Daily Affirmation**

*A single sentence that captures the essence of the story.*

*Contemplate:*

Through this template, the 50 stories transform into 50 practices — 50 inner journeys, 50 mirrors, 50 small awakenings. By the end of the workbook, you will not simply remember the stories — you will *live* them.

### ***Reflection Before You Move Ahead***

Sit for one breath. Feel the quiet inside you. Feel your readiness.

Ask gently:

*"How do I want these stories to change me?"*

Your answer becomes the beginning of the next chapter.

# Phase 2 — Entering the Practice Forest

You are now stepping into the second half of this workbook — a quieter, deeper phase where wisdom moves from the page into your breath, your choices, and the subtle corners of your inner life. Here, the stories of *Whispers of the Zen Forest* become more than teachings. They become companions. Mirrors. Lamps. Invitations.

Each of the 50 stories you are about to explore will guide you inward through eight gentle gateways:

- A summary to help you reconnect with the story's heart
- An emotional check-in to sense what arises in you
- An insightful reflection to reveal your inner patterns
- A Dharma connection to root your understanding in the Buddha's teachings
- A guided mini meditation to settle the teaching into your body
- An embodied practice to live the wisdom in a simple, real-world way
- A journal prompt to open your inner dialogue
- A Zen affirmation to carry into your day like a soft thread of presence

In Phase 1, you *learned* Zen. In Phase 2, you will begin to *live* it. Each template is a small path, and each story is a step. Move slowly. Let the reflections breathe. Let the insights settle. Let these practices become an integral part of your everyday life. As you walk through these 50 pages, remember: Zen does not transform you through force. It transforms you through noticing.

Welcome to Phase 2.

The forest opens here.

# *Before You Begin... (A Gentle Reminder)*

### ***A Note on Repetition and Patience***

As you move through these practices, you may notice that some exercises, meditations, or reflections feel similar—or even nearly the same. Different words, softer turns of phrase, or sometimes no change at all.

This is intentional.

Life rarely presents us with entirely new challenges every day—it repeats lessons until we've truly learned them. The same patterns, different faces. The same tests, new seasons. Mastery in the Zen tradition doesn't come from acquiring endless variation—it grows from meeting the familiar with fresh awareness.

So, if you find yourself thinking, *"Haven't I done this before?"* pause.

Breathe.

And allow the practice to deepen.

Each story invites a new angle, a different layer of insight, a shift in the heart that perhaps wasn't possible the first time. Repetition is not a flaw—it is the training ground for patience, presence, and steady transformation.

May every lesson meet you where you are—and gently carry you one step further.

## Lesson 1: The Wheel That Waited

Riku rushes to carve a wheel, and it collapses. When he slows down, listens, and works with presence, the wheel becomes balanced and steady.

**1. Story Essence**

A lesson in patience, integrity, and mindful action. Use the reminder above to describe the heart of *your* understanding of the story.

*Contemplate:*

**2. Zen Foundation**

This story points toward *wise understanding (paññā), patience, presence, and mindful action.* Choose the Zen principle you feel most strongly reflects.

*Contemplate:*

**3. Teaching Rooted in the Pali Canon**

Suggested direction: The Buddha taught the abandoning of "crookedness and flaws" in bodily, verbal, and mental action.

*Contemplate:*

**4. Mindfulness in Practice**

Suggested direction: Choose a small practice inspired by slowing down — performing one daily action with complete presence.

*Contemplate:*

**5. Reflection Prompts**

Use these prompts to explore the story's message in your own life:

- Where am I rushing to prove something?
- What becomes "wobbly" when I move too fast?
- How does patience change the quality of my work or relationships?
- What does a "wheel that lasts" symbolize for me today?

*Contemplate:*

**6. Gratitude / Compassion / Simplicity Exercise**

Suggested direction: Offer yourself one sentence of compassion for the times you hurried because you felt pressured or afraid.

*Contemplate:*

**7. Mini-Meditation (1–2 Minutes)**

Sit quietly and breathe slowly, imagining your mind becoming as steady and balanced as the finished wheel.

*Contemplate:*

**8. Daily Affirmation**

Suggested affirmation: *"Steadiness grows when I move with presence."*

*Contemplate:*

# *Lesson 2: The Softest Bed*

Haru tries to find warmth and comfort by changing his outer conditions — adding more blankets, straw, and heat. Yet peace arrives only when he quiets his mind.

A lesson in inner refuge, release, and the stillness that brings true rest.

**1. Story Essence**

Recall the heart of this story — Haru's outer struggle and his inner awakening. Describe what feels most meaningful to you.

*Contemplate:*

**2. Zen Foundation**

This story points toward *presence (sati), letting go, stillness, and non-attachment to comfort.* Choose the Zen principle that resonates most deeply for you.

*Contemplate:*

**3. Teaching Rooted in the Pali Canon**

Suggested direction: The Buddha taught that the "fully unbound one sleeps in ease," not because the body is comfortable, but because the mind is free from clinging and disturbance.

*Contemplate:*

**4. Mindfulness in Practice**

Suggested direction: Choose a small practice inspired by mental sweeping—releasing one thought at a time before rest, work, or conversation.

*Contemplate:*

**5. Reflection Prompts**

Use these questions to explore how the story meets your life:

- Where do I try to fix outer conditions while ignoring inner tension?
- What thoughts prevent me from "sleeping in ease"?
- How does letting go—not changing circumstances—bring peace?
- What would a "quiet mind" feel like right now?

*Contemplate:*

**6. Gratitude / Compassion / Simplicity Exercise**

Suggested direction: Offer gratitude to one simple thing that already brings ease — your breath, your body, a moment of quiet, a cup of warm tea.

*Contemplate:*

**7. Mini-Meditation (1–2 Minutes)**

Sit quietly and imagine sweeping your mind clean—one thought, one worry, one regret at a time—like Haru preparing his inner bed.

*Contemplate:*

**8. Daily Affirmation**

Suggested affirmation: *"Ease comes from within me."*

*Contemplate:*

## *Lesson 3: The Cup and the River*

Yuki feels crushed by regret after speaking harshly to a friend. Her teacher shows her that a mistake is like salt — bitter only when held in a small, tight mind. When the heart grows wide like a river, regret dissolves into compassion and clarity.

**1. Story Essence**

Reflect on the emotional movement of the story — from heaviness and guilt to openness and understanding. Describe what stands out most to you.

*Contemplate:*

**2. Zen Foundation**

This story points toward *compassion (karuṇā), non-attachment to guilt, expansion of awareness, and wise understanding.* Choose the Zen principle you feel most strongly awakened.

*Contemplate:*

**3. Teaching Rooted in the Pali Canon**

Suggested direction: The Buddha taught that the results of our actions depend on *how* we hold them — that the spiritual life is possible because the mind can change, expand, and awaken to freedom.

*Contemplate:*

**4. Mindfulness in Practice**

Suggested direction: Choose a small practice inspired by expanding your heart — such as placing your hand on your chest and breathing gently whenever regret appears.

*Contemplate:*

**5. Reflection Prompts**

Use these to sense the story in your own life:

- What "salt" am I holding in a small cup?
- How does regret feel in my body?
- What helps my heart widen instead of tightening?
- How would this situation feel if I approached it like a river?
- What does spaciousness look like in my daily emotional life?

*Contemplate:*

**6. Gratitude / Compassion / Simplicity Exercise**

Suggested direction: Offer compassion to yourself for one past mistake by imagining it dissolving into a wider, kinder space within you.

*Contemplate:*

**7. Mini-Meditation (1–2 Minutes)**

Visualize your mind as a cup becoming a river — widening, softening, flowing — until what was heavy becomes light.

*Contemplate:*

**8. Daily Affirmation**

Suggested affirmation: *"My heart is wide enough to hold and transform anything."*

*Contemplate:*

## *Lesson 4: The Gift That Was Never Taken*

A villager hurls insults at Kento, expecting a reaction. Kento remains calm, receiving nothing. The abbot explains: if a gift is not accepted, it remains with the giver.

**1. Story Essence**

Reflect on the heart of this story — the refusal to pick up anger, the stillness that protects peace. Describe what feels most true or meaningful to you.

*Contemplate:*

**2. Zen Foundation**

This story expresses *non-reactivity, equanimity, emotional non-attachment, and wise understanding (paññā).* Choose the Zen principle that resonates most deeply with your experience.

*Contemplate:*

**3. Teaching Rooted in the Pali Canon**

Suggested direction: The Buddha taught that one should not dwell on the faults or actions of others, but rather on one's own conduct and clarity.

*Contemplate:*

**4. Mindfulness in Practice**

Suggested direction: Choose a practice inspired by Kento's steadiness—such as pausing before reacting, taking one mindful breath, or feeling your feet on the ground when someone speaks harshly.

*Contemplate:*

**5. Reflection Prompts**

Use these questions to illuminate your inner tendencies:

- What "gifts" of anger or criticism do I sometimes accept unconsciously?
- How does my body feel when I take in others' emotions?
- Where can I practice not picking up what isn't mine?
- How would my day change if I paused before reacting?
- What helps me stay steady when someone else is losing balance?

*Contemplate:*

**6. Gratitude / Compassion / Simplicity Exercise**

Suggested direction: Offer yourself a moment of compassion for the times you unknowingly accepted others' emotional burdens.

*Contemplate:*

**7. Mini-Meditation (1–2 Minutes)**

Sit quietly and observe thoughts of anger or harshness arriving like a package — then observe yourself not taking it, letting it remain as it is.

*Contemplate:*

**8. Daily Affirmation**

Suggested affirmation: *"I do not have to pick up what does not belong to me."*

*Contemplate:*

## *Lesson 5: The Farmer and the Snake of Greed*

Jiro discovers a hidden pouch of gold beneath fallen branches. Remembering his teacher's warning — "Do you see that snake?" — he recognizes the danger of greed disguised as opportunity.

**1. Story Essence**

Reflect on the story's emotional movement — temptation arising, wisdom intervening, clarity choosing the higher path. Describe what feels most meaningful to you.

*Contemplate:*

**2. Zen Foundation**

This story emphasizes the importance of *mindful restraint, wise intention, moral clarity (sīla), and discernment through the illusions of desire.* Choose the Zen principle that resonates most strongly with you.

*Contemplate:*

**3. Teaching Rooted in the Pali Canon**

Suggested direction: The Buddha taught that an unwholesome deed is one that brings regret, sorrow, or a "tearful face" after it is done.

*Contemplate:*

**4. Mindfulness in Practice**

Suggested direction: Choose a practice inspired by "looking twice before reaching out your hand"—such as pausing before making any desire-driven decision and checking your intention.

*Contemplate:*

**5. Reflection Prompts**

Explore how this story meets your own life:

- What "snakes" (temptations, impulses, illusions) appear harmless at first glance?
- Where have I acted quickly without pausing to check my intention?
- What does regret feel like in me—and how does wisdom prevent it?
- How would my choices change if I always "looked twice"?
- What inner signs tell me a desire is unwholesome?

*Contemplate:*

**6. Gratitude / Compassion / Simplicity Exercise**

Suggested direction: Offer gratitude to yourself for one moment—past or present—when you chose integrity over temptation.

*Contemplate:*

**7. Mini-Meditation (1–2 Minutes)**

Close your eyes and recall a moment when you were tempted in your life. Breathe gently. When you open your eyes, think about the "snake" beneath the surface — the hidden consequences — and feel the clarity of choosing restraint.

*Contemplate:*

**8. Daily Affirmation**

Suggested affirmation: *"I choose clarity over craving."*

*Contemplate:*

## *Lesson 6: The Treasure Beneath the Dust*

Hiro returns home to a hidden family treasure. Instead of taking the gold, he asks a deeper question: "What good is treasure if it costs me my peace?" Hiro gains a wealth far greater than gold — a heart free from shame and a life rooted in inner richness.

**1. Story Essence**

Reflect on the heart of Hiro's story — the moment he chooses inner peace over material gain. Describe what feels most meaningful to you.

*Contemplate:*

**2. Zen Foundation**

This story highlights the importance of *simplicity, restraint, wise intention, and mindfulness in daily life,* as well as the profound value of inner wealth over external riches. Choose the Zen principle you feel most awakened.

*Contemplate:*

**3. Teaching Rooted in the Pali Canon**

Suggested direction: The Buddha taught that when one is energetic, mindful, pure in thought, speech, and action, and lives according to Dhamma with care, restraint, and right livelihood, "fame and fortune steadily increase."

*Contemplate:*

**4. Mindfulness in Practice**

Suggested direction: Choose a practice that embodies simplicity — such as doing one daily task with complete presence and care, without rushing or seeking reward.

*Contemplate:*

**5. Reflection Prompts**

Use these to explore how this story mirrors your own relationship with desire and peace:

- What forms of "hidden treasure" tempt me in life?
- Where do I trade inner calm for external gain?
- How does simplicity change the quality of my mind and choices?
- What would it mean to live "rich" in peace instead of possessions?
- What treasure has patience already given me?

*Contemplate:*

**6. Gratitude / Compassion / Simplicity Exercise**

Suggested direction: Offer gratitude for one simple aspect of your life that brings you peace — something small, steady, and easily overlooked.

*Contemplate:*

**7. Mini-Meditation (1–2 Minutes)**

Close your eyes and think about lifting a stone (attachment to a scenario) in your own heart — uncovering your "hidden treasure" — then gently setting it down as you choose peace over pressure.

*Contemplate:*

**8. Daily Affirmation**

Suggested affirmation: *"My greatest wealth is the peace I cultivate within."*

*Contemplate:*

## *Lesson 7: The Empty Cup*

Mei arrives holding her husband's ashes, crushed by grief. The monk sends her to find water from a well untouched by sorrow — a well that does not exist. Understanding dissolves isolation, and grief becomes gentler.

**1. Story Essence**

Reflect on the movement from deep sorrow to shared humanity — from isolation to connection, from bitterness to clarity. Describe what feels most meaningful to you.

*Contemplate:*

**2. Zen Foundation**

This story expresses *impermanence (anicca), compassion (karuṇā), shared suffering, and the release of self-centered grief.* Choose the Zen principle awakened most clearly for you.

*Contemplate:*

**3. Teaching Rooted in the Pali Canon**

Suggested direction: The Buddha taught that death comes to all beings before their desires are fulfilled. No life escapes loss. No heart escapes the ache of impermanence.

*Contemplate:*

**4. Mindfulness in Practice**

Suggested direction: Choose a practice inspired by shared humanity — such as offering compassion to yourself *and* to others who have known similar pain.

*Contemplate:*

### 5. Reflection Prompts

Use these questions to soften your understanding of grief:

- Where in my life do I believe my suffering is uniquely mine?
- How does remembering that all beings face loss shift the weight of my pain?
- What happens to bitterness when I feel connected rather than isolated?
- Where can I practise compassion for myself and for others today?
- What "bitter cup" in my life needs to be held with wider understanding?

*Contemplate:*

### 6. Gratitude / Compassion / Simplicity Exercise

Suggested direction: Offer compassion to one memory of loss — gently acknowledging that grief is a sign of love, and that others have walked this path too.

*Contemplate:*

### 7. Mini-Meditation (1–2 Minutes)

Close your eyes and observe your emotions—not erased, but held gently in a wider, more compassionate space. Breathe normally and acknowledge the emotions.

*Contemplate:*

### 8. Daily Affirmation

Suggested affirmation: *"My pain softens when I remember I am not alone."*

*Contemplate:*

## *Lesson 8: The Arrow That Never Flew*

Tama raises his bow to take a life — until an inner voice awakens a deeper truth. In a moment of stillness, he realizes that life is not a target but a shared breath. His greatest "catch" becomes the moment he refused to harm.

**1. Story Essence**

Reflect on the turning point where Tama shifts from instinct to awareness, from taking life to recognizing the interconnectedness of all beings. Describe what resonates most strongly with you.

*Contemplate:*

**2. Zen Foundation**

This story reflects *compassion (karuṇā), non-harming (ahimsa), right intention, and the awakening of inner wisdom.* Choose the Zen principle awakened most clearly for you.

*Contemplate:*

**3. Teaching Rooted in the Pali Canon**

Suggested direction: The Buddha taught that poison does not harm a hand without wounds, just as no evil touches one whose intentions are pure.

*Contemplate:*

**4. Mindfulness in Practice**

Suggested direction: Choose a practice inspired by non-harm, such as pausing to notice when irritation, judgment, or aggression arises and choosing a gentler response.

*Contemplate:*

**5. Reflection Prompts**

Explore how this story mirrors your own intentions:

- Where do I act from habit rather than awareness?
- What "arrows" — words, reactions, judgments — do I aim without pausing?
- What does non-harm mean in my daily interactions?
- How does stillness change the direction of my choices?
- Where is life asking me to lower my metaphorical bow?

*Contemplate:*

**6. Gratitude / Compassion / Simplicity Exercise**

Suggested direction: Offer gratitude for one moment when you chose compassion over impulse — no matter how small.

*Contemplate:*

**7. Mini-Meditation (1–2 Minutes)**

Imagine holding a bow, feeling the tension of reaction — then gently releasing it, letting the arrow fall, and feeling your heart soften. Now, practice gentle breathing and keep your attention on your nostrils.

*Contemplate:*

**8. Daily Affirmation**

Suggested affirmation: *"My intentions guide my actions toward compassion."*

*Contemplate:*

## *Lesson 9: The Bundle at the Gate*

Taro feels crushed by thoughts, feelings, and desires. The teacher makes him carry a heavy bundle — then reveals it was never his to begin with. The burden lifts the moment he realizes he no longer needs to carry what does not belong to him.

**1. Story Essence**

Reflect on the shift from burden to release — from believing everything is "mine" to recognizing the freedom of letting go. Describe what feels most meaningful to you.

*Contemplate:*

**2. Zen Foundation**

This story expresses *letting go, non-attachment (anatta), wise understanding, and the freedom of not identifying with passing mental states.* Choose the Zen principle awakened most clearly for you.

*Contemplate:*

**3. Teaching Rooted in the Pali Canon**

Suggested direction: The Buddha taught that whatever arises from contact with the mind — pleasure, pain, or neither — is *not yours*. Letting go brings long-term happiness.

*Contemplate:*

**4. Mindfulness in Practice**

Suggested direction: Choose a practice inspired by this teaching — such as observing thoughts for one minute and silently noting: "Not mine… it will change… not mine."

*Contemplate:*

**5. Reflection Prompts**

Use these questions to loosen inner clinging:

- What thoughts or feelings do I cling to as “mine”?
- What burdens am I carrying that don’t actually belong to me?
- How does attachment transform passing experiences into enduring memories?
- What happens inside me when I set something down mentally?
- Where can I practice non-identification today?

*Contemplate:*

**6. Gratitude / Compassion / Simplicity Exercise**

Suggested direction: Offer a moment of compassion to yourself for carrying burdens you were never meant to hold.

*Contemplate:*

**7. Mini-Meditation (1–2 Minutes)**

Close your eyes and observe your mind. Then inhale, and exhale, observe the mind alongside. Feel your body soften as the weight leaves your mind.

*Contemplate:*

**8. Daily Affirmation**

Suggested affirmation: *“I release what is not mine to carry.”*

*Contemplate:*

## *Lesson 10: The Lantern That Would Not Stay Lit*

Ryo struggles to stay awake in meditation, fighting his mind's dullness with force. Master Shun teaches him that a fading flame needs care, not pressure. When Ryo stops insisting and starts tending, his inner flame becomes steady and clear.

**1. Story Essence**

Reflect on the shift from struggle to gentleness — from forcing the mind to caring for it like a lantern's flame. Describe the part of the story that feels most meaningful to you.

*Contemplate:*

**2. Zen Foundation**

This story expresses *non-clinging, right effort, mindful adjustment, and compassionate awareness of the mind's changing states.* Choose the Zen principle that resonates most strongly for you.

*Contemplate:*

**3. Teaching Rooted in the Pali Canon**

Suggested direction: The Buddha taught that "nothing is worth insisting on," emphasizing the freedom that comes from releasing rigid expectations.

*Contemplate:*

**4. Mindfulness in Practice**

Suggested direction: Choose a practice inspired by caring for your inner flame — such as shifting posture, walking slowly, refreshing your senses, or mindfully resting when fatigue arises.

*Contemplate:*

**5. Reflection Prompts**

Use these questions to explore your inner effort patterns:

- Where do I force myself instead of tending gently to my mind?
- What happens when I insist on things going a certain way?
- What "flame" in my life needs care instead of pressure?
- How does curiosity change my relationship with difficulty?
- Where can I soften rigid expectations today?

*Contemplate:*

**6. Gratitude / Compassion / Simplicity Exercise**

Suggested direction: Offer compassion to yourself for moments when you fought your own mind instead of caring for it.

*Contemplate:*

**7. Mini-Meditation (1–2 Minutes)**

Sit quietly and imagine your mind as a small lantern. Let the thoughts come and go as they please. On each exhale, feel the tension lifting as the thoughts change.

*Contemplate:*

**8. Daily Affirmation**

Suggested affirmation: *"When I let go of forcing, my inner flame shines naturally."*

*Contemplate:*

## *Lesson 11: The Bowl on the River*

Hana cherished the first bowl she ever crafted, carrying it into monastic life as a part of her identity. Yet the bowl quietly held her to who she had been, rather than who she was becoming. Letting go freed her not from the bowl, but from the burden of the self she no longer needed.

**1. Story Essence**

Reflect on how Hana's attachment to the bowl mirrors the ways we cling to identity, memory, or "mine." Consider the moment she realizes that release is not loss, but rather a return to inner spaciousness.

*Contemplate:*

**2. Zen Foundation**

This story highlights *letting go, non-self (anatta), inner refuge, and freedom from identification.* Choose the Zen principle awakened in you as you reflect.

*Contemplate:*

**3. Teaching Rooted in the Pali Canon**

Suggested direction: The Buddha taught that one is ultimately one's own refuge — not objects, past roles, or identities. Only when the mind stops clinging does it discover the rare refuge that cannot be taken away.

*Contemplate:*

**4. Mindfulness in Practice**

Suggested direction: Choose a small practice related to loosening identity-clinging — noticing one thought that begins with "my" or "mine" today and gently softening its grip.

*Contemplate:*

**5. Reflection Prompts**

Use these prompts to explore the layers of "self" you carry:

- What object, memory, or identity do I cling to as "mine"?
- What tension arises in my body when I imagine loosening that grip?
- How does attachment keep me small or burdened?
- What would spaciousness feel like without that attachment?
- Where else can I still look for refuge?

*Contemplate:*

**6. Gratitude / Compassion / Simplicity Exercise**

Suggested direction: Offer gratitude for one identity or story you can set down, even briefly — not to reject it, but to feel the ease of not holding too tightly.

*Contemplate:*

**7. Mini-Meditation (1–2 Minutes)**

Sit comfortably. Bring attention to the breath at the nostrils. Notice the coolness of the in-breath and the warmth of the out-breath. Observe sensations around the nose and upper lip. If a thought arises, note it gently and return to the breath.

*Contemplate:*

**8. Daily Affirmation**

Suggested affirmation: "*I am free when I release what no longer needs to be carried.*"

*Contemplate:*

## Lesson 12: The Cup with No Handle

Kazuo pauses at Soma's hut and notices a cup without a handle. Soma explains that a handle invites grasping; a handle-less cup teaches careful holding and easy letting go.

**1. Story Essence**

Reflect on how the handle-less cup becomes a symbol for holding people, relationships, and moments without gripping. Consider what this story reveals about motives, expectations, and genuine presence.

*Contemplate:*

**2. Zen Foundation**

This story expresses *non-clinging, simplicity, mindful relationships, and clarity in companionship.* Choose the Zen principle that resonates most with your reflection.

*Contemplate:*

**3. Teaching Rooted in the Pali Canon**

Suggested direction: The Buddha taught that companions driven by motives and impurity are common, and that walking alone — like a rhinoceros — is wiser.

*Contemplate:*

**4. Mindfulness in Practice**

Suggested direction: Choose a small practice related to mindful connection: Notice one interaction today without expecting anything in return — simply meeting the moment as it is.

*Contemplate:*

**5. Reflection Prompts**

Use these to explore your relationship patterns:

- Where in my life do I hold people with grasping or expectation?
- Which relationships feel "handled" — easier to grip than to release?
- How does non-clinging influence the way I present myself to others?
- Where do I choose solitude over clarity rather than avoidance?
- How does it feel when a connection happens without wanting anything?

*Contemplate:*

**6. Gratitude / Compassion / Simplicity Exercise**

Suggested direction: Offer gratitude for one person with whom you share ease — someone you can hold lightly, without grasping.

*Contemplate:*

**7. Mini-Meditation (1–2 Minutes)**

Sit comfortably. Bring attention to the breath at the nostrils. Notice sensations around the upper lip. If the mind wanders, acknowledge it gently and return to the upper lip.

*Contemplate:*

**8. Daily Affirmation**

Suggested affirmation: *"I hold lightly; I meet others without grasping."*

*Contemplate:*

## *Lesson 13: The Ember in the Robe*

Kaito, was shaken during the drought when a merchant falsely accuses the monastery of wrongdoing. Anger rises like a sudden spark, and before he can see clearly, harsh words escape him. By viewing anger as a danger, Kaito begins the path to freedom.

**1. Story Essence**

Reflect on how Kaito moves from irritation to anger, from anger to regret, and from regret to understanding. Consider what part of the story mirrors your own experience with anger.

*Contemplate:*

**2. Zen Foundation**

This story promotes *mindfulness of emotions, restraint, non-reactivity, and wisdom gained from seeing anger clearly.* Choose the Zen principle that resonates most deeply for you.

*Contemplate:*

**3. Teaching Rooted in the Pali Canon**

Suggested direction: The Buddha taught that anger harms the one who indulges it — disturbing the mind, obscuring judgment, and planting seeds of suffering.

*Contemplate:*

**4. Mindfulness in Practice**

Suggested direction: Choose a practice that helps you notice early signs of anger — such as observing bodily sensations the moment irritation arises, before words solidify.

*Contemplate:*

**5. Reflection Prompts**

Use these questions to examine your relationship with anger:

- What does anger feel like in my body before it becomes action?
- How long does its residue stay after I express it?
- What do I lose when anger takes over?
- How does seeing anger as a sensation soften it?
- How can I pause next time the spark appears?

*Contemplate:*

**6. Gratitude / Compassion / Simplicity Exercise**

Suggested direction: Offer gratitude toward yourself for becoming aware of anger, even if the awareness comes after the event.

*Contemplate:*

**7. Mini-Meditation (1–2 Minutes)**

Sit naturally and remain still. Observe sensations arising in the body — heat, tightness, pressure, pulsing, or movement. Notice each sensation as it is, without naming or reacting. Allow sensations to arise and pass, remaining quietly present with the reality of the moment.

*Contemplate:*

**8. Daily Affirmation**

Suggested affirmation: *"When I observe anger clearly, it loses its fire."*

*Contemplate:*

## *Lesson 14: The Archer and the Crow*

Daigo, a master archer with a fierce temper, directs his frustration toward a harmless nun and a crow. His arrow returns as misfortune. The nun responds not with fear or anger, but with compassion, tending to him after he falls.

**1. Story Essence**

Reflect on how Daigo's anger becomes his downfall, and how the nun's compassion reveals the true cost of unwholesome intention. Consider what the story teaches about impulse, intention, and the natural return of one's actions.

*Contemplate:*

**2. Zen Foundation**

This story embodies *non-harm, right intention, compassion, restraint, and the natural consequences of unwholesome actions*. Choose the Zen principle that resonates most deeply with you.

*Contemplate:*

**3. Teaching Rooted in the Pali Canon**

Suggested direction: The Buddha taught that harm directed at one who is pure falls back upon the doer, like dust thrown against the wind. Intention defines consequence more than aim or skill.

*Contemplate:*

**4. Mindfulness in Practice**

Suggested direction: Choose a small practice related to intention: Before speaking or acting today, pause for one breath and notice the intention behind the action.

*Contemplate:*

**5. Reflection Prompts**

Explore your own reactive patterns through these questions:

- When have I acted from irritation or pride and faced the consequences later?
- What sensations arise in me just before I speak or act harshly?
- How does intention shape the results of my actions?
- Where can I choose restraint instead of reaction?
- Who has shown me compassion even when I was in the wrong?

*Contemplate:*

**6. Gratitude / Compassion / Simplicity Exercise**

Suggested direction: Offer compassion toward someone who once acted out of anger toward you — recognizing that they, too, were struck first by their own unwholesome intention.

*Contemplate:*

**7. Mini-Meditation (1–2 Minutes)**

Sit still and upright. Bring awareness to the sensations arising in the mind — such as tightness, heaviness, pain, or movement. Notice how each sensation appears, changes, and fades. Stay with the bare reality of sensations without reacting or judging.

*Contemplate:*

**8. Daily Affirmation**

Suggested affirmation: *"When my intention is pure, my path becomes steady."*

*Contemplate:*

# *Lesson 15: The Potter and the Clay*

Anzu, once a renowned potter, feels age pressing against her craft. But when an apprentice asks her to teach rather than perform, her hands rediscover their memory, and her spirit rediscovers its strength. Falling is not failing.

**1. Story Essence**

Reflect on Anzu's shift from shame to renewal — from believing she had lost her ability to discovering she had only forgotten her purpose. Reflect on what this story teaches about patience, resilience, and self-reflection.

*Contemplate:*

**2. Zen Foundation**

This story expresses *beginner's mind, right effort, resilience, patient mindfulness, and returning to the center after collapse.* Choose the Zen principle that resonates most deeply.

*Contemplate:*

**3. Teaching Rooted in the Pali Canon**

Suggested direction: The Buddha taught to "take delight in mindfulness" and to guard the mind well, for it is mindfulness that lifts one from the mire of discouragement.

*Contemplate:*

**4. Mindfulness in Practice**

Suggested direction: Choose a small practice that mirrors "begin again": When something goes wrong today, pause, breathe, and start again without judgment.

*Contemplate:*

**5. Reflection Prompts**

Explore your relationship with resilience through these reflections:

- Where in my life do I assume it is "too late" to try again?
- What collapses inside me when things go wrong?
- What helps me return to steady effort rather than shame?
- How do I respond when my "first attempt" fails?
- What part of me needs encouragement, not pressure?

*Contemplate:*

**6. Gratitude / Compassion / Simplicity Exercise**

Suggested direction: Offer gratitude to yourself for one thing you have begun again, even after difficulty.

*Contemplate:*

**7. Mini-Meditation (1–2 Minutes)**

Sit upright in a chair, with your hands resting naturally. Let the spine lengthen without strain. Bring gentle awareness to the breath. Notice each breath as a fresh beginning. Stay with simple presence, nothing added, nothing removed.

*Contemplate:*

**8. Daily Affirmation**

Suggested affirmation: *"Each breath is a beginning; I rise again."*

*Contemplate:*

## *Lesson 16: The Five Visitors in the Tea Garden*

Five visitors come seeking tea, but each arrives with inner distortions — pride, inconsistency, gossip, fickleness, and confusion. Genshu meets each with quiet clarity, seeing through their motives without rejecting their humanity.

**1. Story Essence**

Reflect on what each visitor represents — pride, disrespect, gossip, inconsistency, and dullness — and how Genshu stays rooted, steady, and unmoved. Consider what this story teaches about discernment and inner steadiness.

*Contemplate:*

**2. Zen Foundation**

This story expresses *discernment, steadiness, patience, non-reactivity, and clarity of mind in the face of unstable influences.* Choose the Zen principle awakened most clearly for you.

*Contemplate:*

**3. Teaching Rooted in the Pali Canon**

Suggested direction: The Buddha taught that impulsiveness comes from fickle trust and unstable confidence. A mind that constantly shifts cannot see clearly.

*Contemplate:*

**4. Mindfulness in Practice**

Suggested direction: Choose a practice that strengthens steadiness. Today, notice one moment when someone's mood or opinion tries to pull your mind. Gently return to your own clarity before reacting.

*Contemplate:*

**5. Reflection Prompts**

Use these reflections to explore inner stability:

- Which of the five visitors reflects a part of me when I am unsteady?
- Where does my confidence flicker or change too easily?
- How does impulsiveness show up in my decisions or reactions?
- What helps me stay centered when others pull me off balance?
- Where in my life must I stop "drinking from every passing cup"?

*Contemplate:*

**6. Gratitude / Compassion / Simplicity Exercise**

Suggested direction: Offer gratitude for one person in your life who embodies steadiness — someone who doesn't sway with every emotion or story.

*Contemplate:*

**7. Mini-Meditation (1–2 Minutes)**

Sit upright, hands resting in the lap. Let the spine align naturally. Bring gentle awareness to the breath and stay with simple sitting — body still, breath natural, mind aware. If a thought arises, let it pass like a cloud and return to sitting.

*Contemplate:*

**8. Daily Affirmation**

Suggested affirmation: *"I remain steady; I do not drink from every passing mood."*

*Contemplate:*

## Lesson 17: The Five Pebbles of Master Kaien

Mio comes to Master Kaien, burning with hatred toward a fellow monk. Instead of advice, Kaien offers five smooth pebbles — each representing a way to dissolve hatred: goodwill, compassion, equanimity, non-engagement, and recognition of karma.

**1. Story Essence**

Reflect on Mio's anger and how Master Kaien gently transforms it into understanding. Consider which of the five pebbles speaks most strongly to your own emotional patterns.

*Contemplate:*

**2. Zen Foundation**

This story expresses *loving-kindness, compassion, equanimity, wise non-engagement, and insight into karma* — the foundations for dissolving hatred. Choose the Zen principle that resonates most deeply with this story.

*Contemplate:*

**3. Teaching Rooted in the Pali Canon**

Suggested direction: The Buddha taught five methods for subduing hatred: goodwill, compassion, equanimity, non-attachment, and understanding karma, which teaches that each being inherits the results of their actions.

*Contemplate:*

**4. Mindfulness in Practice**

Suggested direction: Choose one "pebble" and practice it today: Goodwill, compassion, equanimity, letting go of attention, or clarity of karma.

*Contemplate:*

**5. Reflection Prompts**

Explore your emotional landscape through these reflections:

- Which "pebble" is hardest for me to hold when I'm angry?
- What story do I tell myself when hatred rises?
- How does my body respond when I soften even slightly?
- How would equanimity impact my relationship with challenging individuals?
- What does it mean to let someone be "heir to their own actions"?

*Contemplate:*

**6. Gratitude / Compassion / Simplicity Exercise**

Suggested direction: Offer goodwill toward someone you find difficult — even one small, sincere wish like "May you be well."

*Contemplate:*

**7. Mini-Meditation (1–2 Minutes)**

Sit upright, hands resting naturally. Do not focus on breath, sensation, or thought. Do not try to change anything. Simply sit — fully present, fully aware, letting everything arise and pass on its own. Nothing to add. Nothing to remove. Just sitting.

*Contemplate:*

**8. Daily Affirmation**

Suggested affirmation: *"Hatred softens when the mind becomes spacious."*

*Contemplate:*

## *Lesson 18: The Two Letters*

Master Yuma responds to Kenta's hurt with two letters — one full of praise, the other full of insult. Kenta feels lifted by one and wounded by the other. Yuma shows him that neither belongs to him. Freedom comes when the mind does not swing.

**1. Story Essence**

Reflect on how Kenta reacts to praise and blame, and how Master Yuma dissolves both with the same quiet fire. Consider what this story teaches about emotional stability and non-reactivity.

*Contemplate:*

**2. Zen Foundation**

This story expresses *equanimity, non-identification, emotional steadiness, and freedom from external validation.* Choose the Zen principle that resonates most deeply with you.

*Contemplate:*

**3. Teaching Rooted in the Pali Canon**

Suggested direction: The Buddha taught not to let insults create bitterness or let praise create excitement.

*Contemplate:*

**4. Mindfulness in Practice**

Suggested direction: Choose a practice that strengthens equanimity When you receive praise or criticism today, pause before reacting. Notice what happens inside you — then let it pass.

*Contemplate:*

**5. Reflection Prompts**

Examine your inner responses to praise and blame:

- Which affects me more deeply — praise or criticism? Why?
- How do I change when others approve of me?
- How do I react when someone disapproves?
- What would it feel like to stay steady in both situations?
- Which "letters" in my life do I still keep opening?

*Contemplate:*

**6. Gratitude / Compassion / Simplicity Exercise**

Suggested direction: Offer gratitude to your own mind for the moments it has stayed steady despite external noise.

*Contemplate:*

**7. Mini-Meditation (1–2 Minutes)**

Sit upright and still. Bring gentle awareness to the natural breath at the nose. Observe sensations as they arise — coolness, warmth, subtle movement. If thoughts, praise, or criticism appear in the mind, notice them and let them pass without engagement. Return to simple sitting.

*Contemplate:*

**8. Daily Affirmation**

Suggested affirmation: *"Praise and blame pass; I remain steady."*

*Contemplate:*

# *Lesson 19: The Bell and the Bees*

Tetsu struggles during meditation as thoughts swarm around him like bees — sweet ones, stinging ones, restless ones. Sister Kano teaches him that the goal is not to destroy the bees but to understand them. If you panic, you get stung. If you observe with steadiness, you can work alongside them.

**1. Story Essence**

Reflect on the shift in Tetsu's understanding — from fighting thoughts to observing them, from fear to familiarity, from chaos to clarity. Consider what this story reveals about the nature of thought.

*Contemplate:*

**2. Zen Foundation**

This story expresses *mindfulness of thoughts, non-reactivity, equanimity, and wise attention.* Choose the Zen principle awakened most clearly.

*Contemplate:*

**3. Teaching Rooted in the Pali Canon**

Suggested direction: The Buddha taught that the master of thought knows which thoughts to cultivate and which to release. Not through suppression, but through awareness.

*Contemplate:*

**4. Mindfulness in Practice**

Suggested direction: When a thought arises today, simply note "thinking," allow it to be, and let it pass without feeding it more attention.

*Contemplate:*

**5. Reflection Prompts**

Use these to explore your relationship with thinking:

- Which thoughts "sting" me the most? Why?
- What happens inside me when I try too hard to control my mind?
- How does noticing a thought (rather than fighting it) change its strength?
- Which thoughts deserve attention? Which do not?
- What would "working beside" my thoughts look like?

*Contemplate:*

**6. Gratitude / Compassion / Simplicity Exercise**

Suggested direction: Offer compassion to yourself for having a busy mind — understanding that thoughts are natural, not a personal failure.

*Contemplate:*

**7. Mini-Meditation (1–2 Minutes)**

Sit still. Notice thoughts as they arise. Acknowledge gently: "thinking." Do not follow the thought. Do not push it away. Let it appear and fade on its own, returning to simple awareness.

*Contemplate:*

**8. Daily Affirmation**

Suggested affirmation: *"I watch my thoughts without fear; they rise and pass."*

*Contemplate:*

## *Lesson 20: The Painted Letter*

Airi, a gifted calligrapher, forges a letter to disgrace the Zen master, believing deception will elevate her. The master responds not with blame, but with a question that cuts deeper than punishment: "Does the heart behind the brush rest easy tonight?"

**1. Story Essence**

Reflect on Airi's transformation — from envy and deceit to humility and willingness to learn. Consider what this story reveals about truth, intention, and inner clarity.

*Contemplate:*

**2. Zen Foundation**

This story expresses *right speech, right intention, honesty, self-awareness, and the purification of the mind through truthfulness.* Choose the Zen principle awakened in you.

*Contemplate:*

**3. Teaching Rooted in the Pali Canon**

Suggested direction: The Buddha warned that one who lies easily becomes capable of all harm. Deception darkens the heart before it harms others.

*Contemplate:*

**4. Mindfulness in Practice**

Suggested direction: Choose a practice that strengthens truthfulness: Today, notice one moment when you are tempted to exaggerate, soften, or distort the truth — and choose clarity instead.

*Contemplate:*

**5. Reflection Prompts**

Use these prompts to look inward gently:

- When have I harmed myself by hiding or bending the truth?
- What feeling drives me toward dishonesty — fear, envy, insecurity?
- What truth in my life needs to be faced rather than avoided?
- How does truth feel in my body compared to deceit?
- What would it mean to keep my "inner water" clear?

*Contemplate:*

**6. Gratitude / Compassion / Simplicity Exercise**

Suggested direction: Offer compassion to yourself for past mistakes made in confusion — and gratitude for the honesty you can choose today.

*Contemplate:*

**7. Mini-Meditation (1–2 Minutes)**

Sit still and upright. Notice any intention that appears in the mind — a pull, a motive, a subtle urge. Acknowledge it gently as "intending." Do not follow it or judge it. Let the intention arise and fade on its own, returning to a state of simple awareness.

*Contemplate:*

**8. Daily Affirmation**

Suggested affirmation: *"Truth clears the mind; I choose clarity."*

*Contemplate:*

## *Lesson 21: The Lantern and the Hot Oil*

Aiko runs her teahouse with warmth and grace. Mariko, her helper, becomes consumed by envy. In a moment of darkness, she lifts a pot of hot oil with the intention to harm or frighten Aiko. But Aiko meets her not with anger, accusation, or fear — but with compassion so deep that it disarms malice at its root.

**1. Story Essence**

Reflect on the moment Aiko turns toward Mariko with calm gratitude instead of fear or anger. Consider how compassion can dissolve harm at its source, even before it reaches the world.

*Contemplate:*

**2. Zen Foundation**

This story expresses *loving-kindness, compassion, disarming harm with goodness, and the strength of non-violence.* Choose the Zen principle that resonates most deeply.

*Contemplate:*

**3. Teaching Rooted in the Pali Canon**

Suggested direction: The Buddha taught that harmful qualities are subdued by their opposites: Anger by loving-kindness, wickedness by goodness, greed by generosity, and falsehood by truth.

*Contemplate:*

**4. Mindfulness in Practice**

Suggested direction: When faced with someone's envy, irritation, or harshness today, pause. Choose one wholesome response—kindness, calmness, or honesty—rather than reacting with the same energy.

*Contemplate:*

**5. Reflection Prompts**

Explore your own patterns through these reflections:

- When have I met harm with harm, and what did it create?
- How would loving-kindness change the outcome of a difficult situation?
- What emotion arises in me when I witness someone else's envy or resentment?
- What inner strength is needed to respond softly instead of reacting sharply?
- Where in my life can I choose a purer intention instead of retaliation?

*Contemplate:*

**6. Gratitude / Compassion / Simplicity Exercise**

Suggested direction: Offer compassion toward someone who once felt envy or resentment toward you — understanding that their suffering came before their action.

*Contemplate:*

**7. Mini-Meditation (1–2 Minutes)**

Sit still and upright. Notice any mental state that arises — irritation, calm, envy, warmth, judgment. Acknowledge it simply as: "anger is present," "envy is present," "kindness is present." Observe the mental state as it arises and fades on its own.

*Contemplate:*

**8. Daily Affirmation**

Suggested affirmation: *"I meet harm with goodness, and goodness grows within me."*

*Contemplate:*

## Lesson 22: The Drums at Dawn

The abbot gently reminded the group of eager novices, who wanted to prove their zeal, by striking three giant drums with thunderous force—disturbing the river, the birds, and the stillness of the morning —that the sunrise doesn't hurry because you are loud. True discipline is quiet. Real strength is inward.

**1. Story Essence**

Contemplate the moment the abbot asks, "Did the sunrise come more quickly because of your noise?" Reflect on how eagerness without awareness becomes disturbance, and how discipline without ego becomes peace.

*Contemplate:*

**2. Zen Foundation**

This story highlights *self-discipline, quiet strength, inner steadiness, and the serenity of true practice.* Choose the Zen principle that aligns with your understanding.

*Contemplate:*

**3. Teaching Rooted in the Pali Canon**

Suggested direction: The Buddha emphasized that the wise are self-controlled in body, speech, and mind.

*Contemplate:*

**4. Mindfulness in Practice**

Suggested direction: Before acting with enthusiasm today, pause and ask: Is this energy steady, or restless? Practice doing one task slowly and silently, allowing intention to guide your effort.

*Contemplate:*

**5. Reflection Prompts**

- Where do I confuse intensity with sincerity?
- When has eagerness turned into disturbance in my life?
- What happens when I let stillness, rather than excitement, lead my actions?
- In what situations do I seek to prove myself, rather than simply practicing?
- What would “a single soft tap” look like in my day?

*Contemplate:*

**6. Gratitude / Compassion / Simplicity Exercise**

Suggested direction: Take one quiet action today—without announcing it, explaining it, or performing it. Let its purity be your gratitude for the stillness of the dawn.

*Contemplate:*

**7. Mini-Meditation (1–2 Minutes)**

Sit still. Notice if the mind feels restless, excited, dull, or calm. Acknowledge the state plainly: “restlessness is present,” “calm is present,” “eagerness is present.” Let the state arise and fade without judgment—simply seeing the mind as mind.

*Contemplate:*

**8. Daily Affirmation**

Suggested affirmation: *“Quiet strength guides my actions.”*

*Contemplate:*

## *Lesson 23: The Three Seeds*

Master Sora planted three dark seeds—greed, aversion, delusion—showing her students how these roots grow tangled vines that choke the heart. Then she set them aside and planted three new seeds—contentment, kindness, clarity—watering them gently in the sunlight.

**1. Story Essence**

Contemplate the transformation from the three dark seeds to the three bright ones. Reflect on the quiet truth that the heart is a garden; it grows what we water.

*Contemplate:*

**2. Zen Foundation**

This story points toward the Zen roots of *clarity, compassion, and the relinquishing of harmful mind-states.* Choose the Zen principle this story awakens for you.

*Contemplate:*

**3. Teaching Rooted in the Pali Canon**

Suggested direction: The Buddha taught that all unskillful actions arise from three roots: greed, aversion, and delusion.

*Contemplate:*

**4. Mindfulness in Practice**

Suggested direction: Today, notice when one of the three unwholesome roots arises: wanting, resisting, or confusion. Gently choose its opposite—contentment, kindness, or clarity—as your response.

*Contemplate:*

**5. Reflection Prompts**

- Which of the three seeds grows most quickly in me—greed, aversion, or delusion?
- How does each root feel in my body?
- What helps me choose contentment over craving?
- What situation in my life needs more kindness?
- Where do I need clearer sight?

*Contemplate:*

**6. Gratitude / Compassion / Simplicity Exercise**

Suggested direction: Offer one small act of kindness—something gentle, quiet, and unannounced. Let it be a seed planted deliberately.

*Contemplate:*

**7. Mini-Meditation (1–2 Minutes)**

Sit quietly. Bring awareness to the breath. With each breath, repeat softly in your mind:

*"May I be free from greed. May I be free from aversion. May I be free from confusion. May my heart grow gentle and clear."*

Let the phrases settle like seeds in warm soil.

*Contemplate:*

**8. Daily Affirmation**

Suggested affirmation: *"I plant contentment, kindness, and clarity in the garden of my heart."*

*Contemplate:*

## *Lesson 24: The Brush and the Flame*

Renji longed to master the brush, yet his strokes twisted with frustration. Master Makoto guided him to the fire pit, showing him, how calm sand makes smooth lines, while wind and haste make jagged ones.

**1. Story Essence**

Contemplate how Renji's brush mirrored the state of his own mind. The flame of anger scorches clarity; the wind of craving shakes the hand. Only a quiet heart creates a steady stroke.

*Contemplate:*

**2. Zen Foundation**

This story expresses the Zen qualities of *right view, mindful action, and calm presence*—skill arising from inner steadiness rather than effort alone. Choose the Zen principle this story inspires in you.

*Contemplate:*

**3. Teaching Rooted in the Pali Canon**

Suggested direction: The Buddha taught that skillful action has roots in contentment, goodwill, and understanding.

*Contemplate:*

**4. Mindfulness in Practice**

Suggested direction: Before beginning any task today—writing, speaking, working—pause for one breath. Ask: "What root is guiding me right now—calm or craving, peace or frustration?" Let the root determine the action.

*Contemplate:*

**5. Reflection Prompts**

- Which "inner flame" most disturbs my stroke—anger, urgency, fear, comparison, craving?
- What does a calm root feel like inside my body?
- How do my actions change when I begin from stillness?
- What is one area of my life that needs more contentment and less striving?

*Contemplate:*

**6. Gratitude / Compassion / Simplicity Exercise**

Suggested direction: Choose one small task today—washing, writing, preparing food—and do it slowly, without rush, as if creating art.

*Contemplate:*

**7. Mini-Meditation (1–2 Minutes)**

Sit comfortably. Bring attention to the breath at the nostrils. Notice the subtle touch of air as it enters and leaves. Observe sensations around the nose, upper lip, or chest. If agitation arises, simply note the sensation where it appears—heat, tightening, pulsing—and return to the breath. Let the breath steady the root.

*Contemplate:*

**8. Daily Affirmation**

Suggested affirmation: *"When my root is calm, my actions become clear and skillful."*

*Contemplate:*

## *Lesson 25: The Lantern Keeper's Way*

Ryuu longed for peace, yet daily life pulled him in many directions. Master Akeno showed him a simple truth while lighting lanterns at dawn: peace is not found by escaping life, but by tending it wisely.

**1. Story Essence**

Contemplate the way Ryuu's confusion softened as he walked the lantern path with Akeno. Each lantern illuminated a part of life that requires mindful tending. The lesson is not to withdraw from life, but to walk through it with steadiness.

*Contemplate:*

**2. Zen Foundation**

This story reflects the spirit of *mindful action, balance, right effort, simplicity, and wise companionship,* showing how the inner and outer worlds support each other when approached with clarity. Choose the Zen principle this story awakens for you.

*Contemplate:*

**3. Teaching Rooted in the Pali Canon**

Suggested direction: The Buddha described four qualities that support a household life rooted in well-being: initiative, protection, good friendship, and balanced finances.

*Contemplate:*

**4. Mindfulness in Practice**

Suggested direction: Choose one of the four lanterns—initiative, protection, friendship, or balance—and bring it into a single action today. Let the act be small, steady, and deliberate, just like lighting one lantern at dawn.

*Contemplate:*

**5. Reflection Prompts**

- Which lantern in my life burns steadily?
- Which one flickers, dims, or is forgotten?
- How do I currently protect what truly matters?
- Who serves as a wholesome companion in my journey?
- Where could I live with more balance and less strain?

*Contemplate:*

**6. Gratitude / Compassion / Simplicity Exercise**

Suggested direction: Think of one person whose presence or example helps steady your life. Offer a silent wish for them: "May your path be bright."

*Contemplate:*

**7. Mini-Meditation (1–2 Minutes)**

Stand naturally. Begin walking slowly, feeling each step through the soles of the feet. Observe sensations—pressure, shifting weight, contact, release. Notice how each sensation arises and passes. If the mind wanders, gently return to lifting, moving, and placing.

*Contemplate:*

**8. Daily Affirmation**

Suggested affirmation: *"I tend the right lights, and life becomes steady."*

*Contemplate:*

## *Lesson 26: The Bamboo Scales*

Two farmers argued fiercely over a piece of land. Master Hoshin asked them each to place their truth—symbolized by a stone—onto a bamboo scale. When both stones were set down, the bamboo balanced perfectly.

**1. Story Essence**

Contemplate how the bamboo balanced when both stories were heard with sincerity. The lesson is not to determine who is right, but to see how each truth can coexist without force or arrogance.

*Contemplate:*

**2. Zen Foundation**

This story reflects *equanimity, right view, non-grasping, and balanced seeing*—the ability to meet conflicting truths with inner stillness rather than reaction. Choose the Zen principle this story awakens for you.

*Contemplate:*

**3. Teaching Rooted in the Pali Canon**

Suggested direction: The Buddha taught that a wise person does not decide by impulse or bias, but rather by examining what is wholesome and what is unwholesome.

*Contemplate:*

**4. Mindfulness in Practice**

Suggested direction: Choose one conversation today to approach without preparing your response in advance. Just listen. Let each "stone" be placed before you without tipping the bamboo of your mind.

*Contemplate:*

**5. Reflection Prompts**

- Where do I tend to "lean" in discussions—toward defensiveness, anger, or pride?
- What does it feel like in my body when I listen without rushing to respond?
- Can I recognize that two truths can exist at once?
- When do I mistake winning for fairness?
- What inner quality allows me to hold both sides without tension?

*Contemplate:*

**6. Gratitude / Compassion / Simplicity Exercise**

Suggested direction: Think of someone with whom you've disagreed recently. Offer a silent sentence: "May I see your truth without grasping my own."

*Contemplate:*

**7. Mini-Meditation (1–2 Minutes)**

Sit upright and still. Let the body settle naturally. Do not follow thoughts or push them away. Allow sounds, sensations, and passing emotions to arise and fade naturally. Sit as the bamboo: present, steady, straight.

*Contemplate:*

**8. Daily Affirmation**

Suggested affirmation: *"I meet every truth with balance and a steady heart."*

*Contemplate:*

## *Lesson 27: The Bell of Clear Knowing*

During a festival of competing teachers, each proclaimed their way as the only path. But the old nun Ema brought no chants, no rituals, no doctrines—only a simple bell. She taught the villagers to listen not to claims, but to the *inner bell* of clear knowing:

**1. Story Essence**

Contemplate the old nun's simplicity as she cut through noise and confusion with a single sound. The story teaches that truth is not inherited from tradition or authority—it is recognized through your own direct experience.

*Contemplate:*

**2. Zen Foundation**

This story conveys *wise understanding (paññā), self-inquiry, direct knowing, and non-attachment to views*—the courage to look for yourself rather than borrow certainty from others. Choose the Zen principle this story awakens for you.

*Contemplate:*

**3. Teaching Rooted in the Pali Canon**

Suggested direction: The Buddha advised not to rely on scripture, tradition, logic, or authority. Instead, he urged practitioners to examine qualities directly—"If they lead to harm and suffering, abandon them."

*Contemplate:*

**4. Mindfulness in Practice**

Suggested direction: When someone makes a strong claim today—about you, the world, what you "must" do, or what is "right"—pause.

*Contemplate:*

**5. Reflection Prompts**

- When have I accepted something as truth without checking it against my own experience?
- What signs tell me that a teaching or idea is "true enough" for me to walk with?
- What does inner clarity feel like in my body?
- Which voices in my life trigger confusion—and which awaken peace?
- How often do I mistake confidence for wisdom?

*Contemplate:*

**6. Gratitude / Compassion / Simplicity Exercise**

Suggested direction: Think of someone who once spoke a truth that landed gently and clearly in your heart. Offer a silent gratitude: "Thank you for the clarity you helped me see."

*Contemplate:*

**7. Mini-Meditation (1–2 Minutes)**

Sit comfortably. Let the body settle. Observe sensations in the chest, stomach, or throat as they naturally arise—tightness, ease, warmth, pulsing, softening. Notice how each sensation changes moment by moment. Allow clarity to come not through thought, but through direct experience of what is happening right now.

*Contemplate:*

**8. Daily Affirmation**

Suggested affirmation: *"I listen for the truth that rings clear in my own heart."*

*Contemplate:*

## *Lesson 28: The Pot of Ink*

Every night, two novices debate the Dharma passionately—loudly, fervently, eager to prevail. Their fight woke the old caretaker up. Yorin shows them a pot of black ink. "Whether you write a blessing or an insult," he says, "the ink remains the same."

**1. Story Essence**

This story reveals how easily noble words can become weapons when spoken with anger or pride. Clarity returns when you talk with humility rather than certainty.

*Contemplate:*

**2. Zen Foundation**

This story expresses *right speech, inner clarity, humility, mindful communication, and non-contention.* Choose the Zen principle this story awakens for you.

*Contemplate:*

**3. Teaching Rooted in the Pali Canon**

Suggested direction: The Buddha warns against speaking when angered, arrogant, or eager to expose faults. Such speech is not the way of the noble ones.

*Contemplate:*

**4. Mindfulness in Practice**

Suggested direction: Today, before entering a discussion—whether gentle or heated—pause for one breath. Ask: "Am I speaking to understand, or to win?" Let this awareness soften your tone and steady your heart.

*Contemplate:*

**5. Reflection Prompts**

- When have I spoken with the intention of proving myself rather than understanding?
- What happens in my body when I argue from pride or irritation?
- How do I feel after conversations where I "win" but do not grow?
- Which relationships in my life need clearer, quieter speech?
- What does skillful speech mean to me today?

*Contemplate:*

**6. Gratitude / Compassion / Simplicity Exercise**

Suggested direction: Recall someone who once spoke to you with patience, even when you were difficult. Offer gratitude in silence: "Thank you for not darkening the moment with anger."

*Contemplate:*

**7. Mini-Meditation (1–2 Minutes)**

Sit quietly. Bring awareness to subtle sensations around the chest, throat, and face. Notice any tension or warmth that arises when recalling a recent conversation. Observe each sensation without judgment—simply feeling the body as it is. Let the sensations rise and pass naturally.

*Contemplate:*

**8. Daily Affirmation**

Suggested affirmation: *"I speak from clarity, not from the need to be right."*

*Contemplate:*

## *Lesson 29: The Four Ways to Answer*

Four visitors asked Master Koji four very different questions. He answered one with a clear no, one with a gentle explanation, one with a question, and one with silence. Each response matched the nature of the inquiry

**1. Story Essence**

This story teaches that not all questions deserve the same response. Some require clarity, some require guidance, some require reflection, and some require silence.

*Contemplate:*

**2. Zen Foundation**

This story expresses *wise discernment, right view, skillful means, and mindful speech.* Choose the Zen principle this story awakens for you.

*Contemplate:*

**3. Teaching Rooted in the Pali Canon**

Suggested direction: The Buddha taught that a wise person distinguishes between what is worthwhile and what is not, rejecting the unhelpful and embracing the meaningful.

*Contemplate:*

**4. Mindfulness in Practice**

Suggested direction: Before responding to a question today—spoken or unspoken—pause and ask: "Is this worth answering? And what is the most skillful way to answer?" Let discernment guide your words.

*Contemplate:*

**5. Reflection Prompts**

- When do I answer out of habit rather than wisdom?
- Which questions in my life lead only to confusion or anxiety?
- When have I needed silence instead of explanation?
- Which inquiries help me grow—and which keep me stuck?
- How do I know internally when something is "worthwhile"?

*Contemplate:*

**6. Gratitude / Compassion / Simplicity Exercise**

Suggested direction: Think of someone who once gave you an answer that changed you—whether direct, gentle, reflective, or silent. Silently thank them for the wisdom of their discernment.

*Contemplate:*

**7. Mini-Meditation (1–2 Minutes)**

Sit quietly. Observe thoughts as they arise—questions, commentary, fragments of speech. Note each one simply as "thinking" without following it. Let it pass. Return to the bare knowing of the present moment and remember that everything passes.

*Contemplate:*

**8. Daily Affirmation**

Suggested affirmation: *"I respond with clarity, and I release what is not worthwhile."*

*Contemplate:*

## *Lesson 30: The Empty Teacup*

"Like praise into a swollen heart," the master Senzō says to Tomo, "Even truth becomes distorted when the mind seeks admiration." Only an empty cup can truly receive tea.

**1. Story Essence**

This story reveals the quiet danger of conceit, subtle pride, and the craving for recognition. Tomo thinks he speaks truth, but the truth bends under the weight of his self-image. Master Senzō shows that humility is not weakness—it is the empty vessel through which clarity flows.

*Contemplate:*

**2. Zen Foundation**

This story *embodies non-self (anattā), a beginner's mind, humility, right speech, and the letting go of conceit.* Choose the Zen principle this story awakens for you.

*Contemplate:*

**3. Teaching Rooted in the Pali Canon**

Suggested direction: The Buddha taught: do not be led into lying, infatuation with form, or hasty conduct. Pride, conceit, and the desire to be admired cloud perception.

*Contemplate:*

**4. Mindfulness in Practice**

Suggested direction: Before speaking today, pause and ask: "Am I speaking to express truth—or to be seen as truthful?" Let your intention settle. Speak only from the part of you that is quiet and sincere.

*Contemplate:*

**5. Reflection Prompts**

- Where in my life is my "cup" too full for new understanding?
- When do I speak to impress rather than to connect or help?
- What does humility feel like in my body?
- How does praise affect my behavior?
- What would it mean to "empty the cup" in my daily life?

*Contemplate:*

**6. Gratitude / Compassion / Simplicity Exercise**

Suggested direction: Recall one truth you resisted at first but eventually accepted. Instead of analyzing it, simply acknowledge it with a quiet breath. Let this moment remind you that clarity grows when you soften and return to what is simple.

*Contemplate:*

**7. Mini-Meditation (1–2 Minutes)**

Sit still. Bring attention to sensations in the face, chest, or stomach as you recall a recent moment of pride or defensiveness. Notice tightening, warmth, pulsing, or shifting sensations. Observe each sensation without judgment until it changes or fades.

*Contemplate:*

**8. Daily Affirmation**

Suggested affirmation: *"I empty my cup so truth can enter."*

*Contemplate:*

## *Lesson 31: The Persimmon Tree*

Isamu disliked correction, even when it was kind. The persimmon tree became a mirror—teaching that rebuke from a wise teacher is not harm but guidance. When we stop guarding our faults, real growth becomes possible.

**1. Story Essence**

This story reveals how defensiveness hides our greatest growth opportunities. Isamu resists feedback, but Genjo shows him—through the treasure map—that true treasure is hidden beneath the very resistance he avoids.

*Contemplate:*

**2. Zen Foundation**

This story expresses *right effort, humility, wise friendship, openness to guidance, and the courage to see one's flaws clearly.* Choose the Zen principle this story awakens for you.

*Contemplate:*

**3. Teaching Rooted in the Pali Canon**

Suggested direction: The Buddha taught that one should follow a wise person who points out faults as eagerly as one would seek buried treasure. The treasure is not gold—it is inner honesty.

*Contemplate:*

**4. Mindfulness in Practice**

Suggested direction: Today, when someone offers feedback—no matter how small—pause. Let the first reaction soften. Ask silently: "What treasure might be beneath this discomfort?"

*Contemplate:*

**5. Reflection Prompts**

- Where do I resist correction, even when it could help me?
- What sensations arise when someone points out my mistakes?
- What would it feel like to treat wise critique as treasure?
- Which areas of my life need more humility and openness?
- How do I distinguish between harmful criticism and helpful guidance?

*Contemplate:*

**6. Gratitude / Compassion / Simplicity Exercise**

Suggested direction: Recall one recent correction someone gave you. Instead of defending or justifying, simply acknowledge it with one breath. Let simplicity open a small space for insight.

*Contemplate:*

**7. Mini-Meditation (1–2 Minutes)**

Sit comfortably. Recall a moment of receiving correction. Observe sensations in the body—such as tightness, heat, shifting, and restlessness. Do not analyze or judge. Let sensations arise and pass, noticing how resistance loosens when observed with clarity.

*Contemplate:*

**8. Daily Affirmation**

Suggested affirmation: *"I welcome corrections that guide me toward clarity."*

*Contemplate:*

## *Lesson 32: The Tale of the Complaining Visitors*

The villagers complain about every teacher—too silent, too talkative, too simple. The Zen master finally reveals: "The fault-finding mind will never be at peace."

**1. Story Essence**

This story teaches that complaints say more about the complainer than the world. No teacher pleased the villagers because their minds were tuned toward fault, not truth. Peace begins when we stop measuring, comparing, and criticizing everything we meet.

*Contemplate:*

**2. Zen Foundation**

This story reflects *equanimity, humility, right view, non-judgment, beginner's mind, contentment, and simplicity.* Choose the Zen principle this story awakens for you.

*Contemplate:*

**3. Teaching Rooted in the Pali Canon**

Suggested direction: The Buddha taught that blame and praise are inevitable, even for the wise and the awakened. Wisdom is not about avoiding criticism—it is about recognizing which judgments matter, and which arise from confusion.

*Contemplate:*

**4. Mindfulness in Practice**

Suggested direction: For one day, when your mind says, "too much, too little, not enough," pause. Ask gently: "Is this about the world—or my restlessness?" Notice how often complaint arises without necessity.

*Contemplate:*

**5. Reflection Prompts**

- What conditions make my mind quick to blame or criticize?
- How often do I blame because I am uncomfortable, not because something is wrong?
- Which form of teaching do I resist—silence, depth, or simplicity?
- When has a complaint closed the door to learning?
- What would it feel like to listen without seeking faults?

*Contemplate:*

**6. Gratitude / Compassion / Simplicity Exercise**

Suggested direction: Choose one recurring complaint you carry today. Release it for one breath. Let the mind grow just a little more spacious.

*Contemplate:*

**7. Mini-Meditation (1–2 Minutes)**

Sit quietly and observe any thoughts that involve judgment, comparison, or blame. Do not push it away; observe the sensation it produces—tightness, heat, pressure, contraction. See how the thought and the sensation both arise and pass naturally when not fed.

*Contemplate:*

**8. Daily Affirmation**

Suggested affirmation: *"When I release complaint, wisdom becomes easier to hear."*

*Contemplate:*

## *Lesson 33: The Lantern of a Simple Heart*

Lian makes simple lanterns. People criticize her—too plain, too dull, too old-fashioned. But she tends her lanterns quietly, without arguing or defending. "My lantern's light does not depend on who approves," she says.

**1. Story Essence**

This story reveals the ease with which people judge others—while remaining blind to their own projections. Lian's lanterns shine simply because she tends them with sincerity, not because anyone approves. Fault-finding clouds vision; sincerity clears it.

*Contemplate:*

**2. Zen Foundation**

This story embodies *equanimity, simplicity, inner steadiness, non-judgment, and mindful action without attachment to praise or blame*. Choose the Zen principle this story awakens for you.

*Contemplate:*

**3. Teaching Rooted in the Pali Canon**

Suggested direction: The Buddha taught that it is easy to see the faults of others but difficult to see one's own.

*Contemplate:*

**4. Mindfulness in Practice**

Suggested direction: When someone criticizes you today—silently or aloud—pause. Ask quietly: "Is their opinion a truth… or just a passing shadow?" Return to what you are tending with sincerity.

*Contemplate:*

**5. Reflection Prompts**

- When have I allowed others' opinions to dim my inner light?
- Which judgments from others do I carry unnecessarily?
- What does my "lantern" look like—simple, quiet, sincere?
- How often do I judge others without understanding them?
- What would it feel like to act without seeking approval?

*Contemplate:*

**6. Gratitude / Compassion / Simplicity Exercise**

Suggested direction: Take one small task today—brewing tea, folding cloth, sweeping, writing—and do it without seeking praise or validation. Let the act be complete in itself.

*Contemplate:*

**7. Mini-Meditation (1–2 Minutes)**

Sit naturally. Let the body settle. Do not control the breath. Do not follow thoughts. Do not try to fix anything. Simply sit, open and present, like a lantern that shines by its own nature.

*Contemplate:*

**8. Daily Affirmation**

Suggested affirmation: *"My light shines because I tend it with sincerity."*

*Contemplate:*

## *Lesson 34: The Potter's Bowl*

Taiga brings a cracked bowl to Master Minato, grieving what he has "lost." The master shows him that the bowl was always empty—of rice, of water, of flowers—emptiness was its true nature. The crack doesn't remove the emptiness; it only makes it visible.

**1. Story Essence**

This story invites us to see emptiness not as brokenness but as spaciousness. The crack reveals what was always there—the openness that makes all things usable, lovable, and ever-new. Nothing truly "lost" was ever fixed in the first place.

*Contemplate:*

**2. Zen Foundation**

This story awakens *the insight of emptiness (non-self), simplicity, non-clinging, and the freedom of beginning again.* Choose the Zen principle this story awakens for you.

*Contemplate:*

**3. Teaching Rooted in the Pali Canon**

Suggested direction: The Buddha taught that we regard each thing as "empty of what is not there," and understand clearly "what remains"—the truth of its nature.

*Contemplate:*

**4. Mindfulness in Practice**

Suggested direction: Hold an object today—a cup, a bowl, a pen—and notice what it *is* and what it *is not.* Let this simple observation loosen your clinging to how things "should" remain.

*Contemplate:*

**5. Reflection Prompts**

- What am I grieving today that may not have been "mine" to hold?
- What cracks in my life are revealing a deeper spaciousness?
- Where do I mistake change for loss?
- How would it feel to meet the present moment without clinging?

*Contemplate:*

**6. Gratitude / Compassion / Simplicity Exercise**

Suggested direction: Choose one small expectation—of life, of someone, of yourself—and loosen your grip on it. Let the moment be wide and unforced, like a bowl that holds whatever comes.

*Contemplate:*

**7. Mini-Meditation (1–2 Minutes)**

Sit comfortably. Let the breath move on its own. Feel the body simply here. Notice the space around sensations—the gaps, the openness. Rest in that natural spaciousness without adding or removing anything.

*Contemplate:*

**8. Daily Affirmation**

Suggested affirmation: *"I rest in spaciousness; nothing is lost, everything begins anew."*

*Contemplate:*

## *Lesson 35: The Five Pebbles*

Kenzo shows Aoto five stones—each shaped by time, tide, distance, inner cracks, and hidden weight. Through them, he reveals a simple truth: everything changes, everything transforms, and our actions alone endure.

**1. Story Essence**

This story reminds us that life shapes us—through aging, hardship, movement, unseen fractures—and yet what truly remains is the imprint of our actions. When we see this clearly, we cling less, appreciate more, and live with gentle integrity.

*Contemplate:*

**2. Zen Foundation**

This story awakens the principles of *impermanence, mindful action, karma-awareness, simplicity, and wise understanding*. Choose the Zen principle this story awakens for you.

*Contemplate:*

**3. Teaching Rooted in the Pali Canon**

Suggested direction: The Buddha taught that all beings are "owners of their actions, heirs to their actions," carried by them as surely as stones carried by the sea.

*Contemplate:*

**4. Mindfulness in Practice**

Suggested direction: Pick up a stone, shell, or simple household object. Observe its marks, color, weight, and texture. Let it remind you that you, too, have been shaped by time and choices—both your own and life's tides. Notice what this recognition softens within you.

*Contemplate:*

**5. Reflection Prompts**

- Which "pebble" from Kenzo's five mirrors a season of my own life?
- What cracks or changes do I hide that are simply part of being human?
- How do my daily actions become the legacy I inherit?
- What small, skillful act can I choose today?

*Contemplate:*

**6. Gratitude / Compassion / Simplicity Exercise**

Suggested direction: Do one small act today with complete honesty and presence—no embellishment, no rush, no expectation—just the clean intention of a clear heart.

*Contemplate:*

**7. Mini-Meditation (1–2 Minutes)**

Sit with the body still. Notice one sensation—pressure, warmth, coolness, tightness. Watch it arise, change, dissolve. Let this remind you that all experiences pass…

*Contemplate:*

**8. Daily Affirmation**

Suggested affirmation: *"My actions shape my path; each moment is a chance to begin cleanly."*

*Contemplate:*

## *Lesson 36: The Bamboo Test*

Jun believed he understood meditation, yet he missed its essence—until silence and bamboo taught him what no scroll could: wisdom requires watching the mind, not just its methods.

**1. Story Essence**

Jun was prideful and restless, clinging to techniques and accomplishments. Through the quiet presence of bamboo, he finally saw the source of his suffering—his own unexamined mind. In stillness, he discovered humility and true inner observation.

*Contemplate:*

**2. Zen Foundation**

This story awakens the principles of *self-inquiry, quiet observation, humility, presence, and non-striving.* Choose the Zen principle this story awakens for you.

*Contemplate:*

**3. Teaching Rooted in the Pali Canon**

Suggested direction: The Buddha advised that you should be skilled in reading your own mind. Meditation is not the display of endurance or technique—it is the steady turning inward, the willingness to sit with restlessness and see its roots without judgment.

*Contemplate:*

**4. Mindfulness in Practice**

Suggested direction: Place a natural object before you—a leaf, a stone, a stick. Sit with it for 3–5 minutes. See where the mind rushes, criticizes, or grows impatient. Each time, gently return to the object without expectation—like bamboo, simply being.

*Contemplate:*

**5. Reflection Prompts**

- What am I trying to prove in my practice or life?
- Can I sit still long enough to see what I've been avoiding?
- Where in my mind is restlessness hiding?
- How can I practice without needing recognition?

*Contemplate:*

**6. Gratitude / Compassion / Simplicity Exercise**

Suggested direction: Take a moment to thank the part of you that still shows up, even when restless. Place a hand over your heart. Say gently: "Thank you for trying."

*Contemplate:*

**7. Mini-Meditation (1–2 Minutes)**

Sit quietly with eyes gently lowered. Notice thoughts as they arise—not to control or eliminate, but to know: *"thinking"... "planning"... "resisting"... "judging."* Note each softly, then let it pass like a cloud. Do not dwell on why.

*Contemplate:*

**8. Daily Affirmation**

Suggested affirmation: *"The quieter I become, the more clearly I see."*

*Contemplate:*

## *Lesson 37: Just This*

Naoki searched for enlightenment across mountains and teachings, only to discover it in washing a bowl—when the wanderer told him to simply see what is seen simply, feel what is felt, and leave it at that. No clinging, no escaping—just this.

**1. Story Essence**

This story reminds us that peace does not come from seeking more, but from seeing clearly what's already here. When we strip away stories, labels, and judgments, each moment becomes complete in itself.

*Contemplate:*

**2. Zen Foundation**

This story awakens the principles of *presence, non-clinging, simplicity, direct perception, and mindful awareness.* Choose the Zen principle this story awakens for you.

*Contemplate:*

**3. Teaching Rooted in the Pali Canon**

Suggested direction: The Buddha taught that, in reference to what is seen, heard, sensed, or thought, let there be only the bare experience, without additions or interpretations. This is the gateway to freedom from clinging.

*Contemplate:*

**4. Mindfulness in Practice**

Suggested direction: While washing dishes, opening a window, or walking slowly, let the experience be simply what it is—color, sound, and movement. No stories. No judgment. Just this moment, exactly as it is.

*Contemplate:*

**5. Reflection Prompts**

- Where in my day do I add too much meaning to what is simple?
- What happens when I allow experience to be just itself?
- How does removing commentary change my relationship to the moment?
- What part of my life could soften if I stopped naming and analyzing long enough to simply witness?

*Contemplate:*

**6. Gratitude / Compassion / Simplicity Exercise**

Suggested direction: Today, choose one ordinary task—drinking tea, washing hands, or watching the sky. Do it as if it were the first and only time, with full attention and no mental commentary.

*Contemplate:*

**7. Mini-Meditation (1–2 Minutes)**

Sit quietly with your eyes open or closed. Notice the breath as it enters and leaves—no labeling, no controlling, just presence. When the mind wanders, notice it and gently bring your attention back to the breath. This is just this moment, as it is.

*Contemplate:*

**8. Daily Affirmation**

Suggested affirmation: *"Just this moment is enough."*

*Contemplate:*

## *Lesson 38: The Tale of the Bitter Fruits*

Two neighbors, fueled by resentment, fed a bitter cycle of revenge year after year. The fruit of their bitterness grew only more bitter—until a visiting teacher reminded them that what they water, they will taste.

**1. Story Essence**

This story reminds us that resentment is a seed we continually nurture within ourselves. Every act of retaliation reinforces the bitterness we claim to despise. When we stop feeding anger with more anger, the cycle breaks, and peace takes root.

*Contemplate:*

**2. Zen Foundation**

This story awakens the principles *of loving-kindness (metta), non-enmity, compassion, mindful choice, and breaking cycles of harm.* Choose the Zen principle this story awakens for you.

*Contemplate:*

**3. Teaching Rooted in the Pali Canon**

Suggested direction: The Buddha taught that hatred is never appeased by hatred; only loving-kindness can end enmity. The moment we choose goodwill over retaliation; we step out of the cycle of suffering.

*Contemplate:*

**4. Mindfulness in Practice**

Suggested direction: When resentment arises today, pause. Instead of reacting, place your hand gently over your heart. Breathe in slowly and silently offer: *"May I be free from resentment. May they be free from suffering."* Let this gesture become a doorway to peace rather than another act of watering bitterness.

*Contemplate:*

**5. Reflection Prompts**

- What "bitter fruits" have I been tasting in my own life?
- Where am I still watering an old grudge without realizing it?
- How does it feel, even briefly, to wish well for someone I've resented?
- What might loving-kindness interrupt that revenge cannot?

*Contemplate:*

**6. Gratitude / Compassion / Simplicity Exercise**

Suggested direction: Do one small kindness (even silently) for someone you have resented. Don't announce it. Let your heart soften through action, not words.

*Contemplate:*

**7. Mini-Meditation (1–2 Minutes)**

Sit upright. Feel the breath rise and fall naturally. With each in-breath, notice the body. With each out-breath, feel tension dissolve. If resentment appears, simply name it "anger," then return to the breath. Let presence break the pattern.

*Contemplate:*

**8. Daily Affirmation**

Suggested affirmation: *"I choose what I water—today, I will water peace."*

*Contemplate:*

## Lesson 39: The Bamboo and the Bell

When Ren witnessed another monk taking rice, he rushed to accuse him. But his master taught him: truth without temper is noise; truth with care becomes a bell that wakes compassion.

**1. Story Essence**

This story teaches us that speaking truth demands not only honesty but also composure. A sharp tongue may ring, but only a steady heart resonates clearly. When grounded in care, truth becomes an awakening—not a weapon.

*Contemplate:*

**2. Zen Foundation**

This story awakens the principles of *truthfulness, equanimity, wise speech, compassion, and mindful action*. Choose the Zen principle this story awakens for you.

*Contemplate:*

**3. Teaching Rooted in the Pali Canon**

Suggested direction: The Buddha taught that even when accused—whether rightly or wrongly—one should ground oneself in two things: truth and an even temper. Only then does truth become liberating, not destructive.

*Contemplate:*

**4. Mindfulness in Practice**

Suggested direction: Before giving feedback or speaking up, pause. Place your hand lightly on your belly, breathe slowly, and silently ask: "Is my voice steady? Is my intention clear?" Wait until your heart feels as calm as a still bell before you speak.

*Contemplate:*

**5. Reflection Prompts**

- When have I rung a bell too harshly, even if I was right?
- What does "truth with care" mean in my relationships?
- Am I more eager to be correct or to be helpful?
- Who in my life could benefit from hearing truth spoken with softness?

*Contemplate:*

**6. Gratitude / Compassion / Simplicity Exercise**

Suggested direction: Offer a sincere, gentle acknowledgment to someone you've judged silently—either through a message, a gesture, or a quiet blessing in your heart.
*Contemplate:*

**7. Mini-Meditation (1–2 Minutes)**

Sit comfortably. Feel the breath rise and fall. Notice the first sensation in the body—tightness, warmth, or tingling. Let it soften as you breathe. With each exhale, mentally whisper: "Steady… clear…" End when the breath and mind feel balanced.
*Contemplate:*

**8. Daily Affirmation**

Suggested affirmation: *"I speak truth gently, with a calm heart."*
*Contemplate:*

## *Lesson 40: The Friend in the Storm*

Osamu walks through rain and hardship to bring warmth to Kaito—an act of presence that speaks louder than any teachings. Through him, we glimpse the true measure of friendship: steadfastness in storm, and silence filled with care.

**1. Story Essence**

This story reveals the heart of true friendship—not in convenience or comfort, but in weathering storms together. Real devotion is quiet, consistent, and grounded, not in need or gain, but in presence.

*Contemplate:*

**2. Zen Foundation**

This story awakens the principles of *compassion, loyalty, generosity, mindful presence, and unconditional support*. Choose the Zen principle this story awakens for you.

*Contemplate:*

**3. Teaching Rooted in the Pali Canon**

Suggested direction: The Buddha said that a true friend offers what is difficult to give, stays when others leave, and remains steadfast when misfortune strikes. Such a friend is to be cherished as a blessing.

*Contemplate:*

**4. Mindfulness in Practice**

Suggested direction: Offer a quiet presence to someone today. Not to fix, not to advise—simply to sit with them, listen, or share space. Let your comfort come from your calm presence, not your words.

*Contemplate:*

**5. Reflection Prompts**

- Who has walked through the rain for me when I felt most alone?
- When was the last time I offered a silent presence rather than a solution?
- What makes kindness feel effortless from a true friend?
- How can I cultivate friendships that endure storms rather than just sunny days?

*Contemplate:*

**6. Gratitude / Compassion / Simplicity Exercise**

Suggested direction: Write a short note—or send a silent blessing—to someone who has stayed by your side when you offered nothing in return.

*Contemplate:*

**7. Mini-Meditation (1–2 Minutes)**

Sit comfortably. Feel the weight of your body and the support beneath you. Notice any sensation in your chest or belly. Breathe gently, letting each inhale soften, and each exhale steady you. End by silently repeating: “I am here. I stay.”

*Contemplate:*

**8. Daily Affirmation**

Suggested affirmation: *“I honor the friends who stay—and I choose to be one of them.”*

*Contemplate:*

## Lesson 41: The Lantern Festival

Shuta hesitates to write his wish during the Lantern Festival—unsure of what blessing to ask for. The old Zen master recalls a child who once wished: *"May no one be afraid of me."* Through this, a deeper truth shines: the most powerful wish is to walk this world without causing fear, harm, or sorrow.

**1. Story Essence**

This story uncovers the gentle strength in choosing kindness over personal gain. True peace shines not from grand achievements, but from a presence that brings safety, ease, and trust wherever it goes.

*Contemplate:*

**2. Zen Foundation**

This story awakens the principles of *non-harm (ahiṃsā), loving-kindness (mettā), mindful speech, compassion, and humility.* Choose the Zen principle this story awakens for you.

*Contemplate:*

**3. Teaching Rooted in the Pali Canon**

Suggested direction: The Buddha taught that one should not wish harm on others—not in thought, word, or action—and that peace arises when our presence inspires no fear.

*Contemplate:*

**4. Mindfulness in Practice**

Suggested direction: Spend a few moments today practicing non-threatening presence. As you speak, walk, or enter a space, ask: Am I a source of calm or tension? Did others feel safe around me? Let this awareness guide your behavior gently.

*Contemplate:*

**5. Reflection Prompts**

- What effect does my presence have on others—spoken or silent?
- When was the last time I wished to be *understood* rather than *considered right*?
- Who in my life feels safe with me—and why?
- What would it look like to be someone no one fears?

*Contemplate:*

**6. Gratitude / Compassion / Simplicity Exercise**

Suggested direction: Think of someone who has made you feel safe. Send them a silent wish: May you be at ease. May your kindness multiply. Then practice that quality toward someone else today.

*Contemplate:*

**7. Mini-Meditation (1–2 Minutes)**

Sit comfortably. Notice the breath entering and leaving the body. With each inhale, silently say: "May I be calm." With each exhale, silently say: "May I bring peace." Let this become your lantern—steady, humble, and bright.

*Contemplate:*

**8. Daily Affirmation**

Suggested affirmation: *"May my presence be light and my heart be safe for others."*

*Contemplate:*

## *Lesson 42: The Two Cups*

Ichirō, a humble potter, meets two visitors: One demands perfection without offering thanks, the other returns a broken cup with genuine gratitude. Gratitude—like a glaze—turns even the ordinary into something luminous.

**1. Story Essence**

This story highlights the quiet difference between entitlement and gratitude. What defines the worth of a gift isn't flawlessness, but the heart with which it's received. Gratitude doesn't wait for perfection—it sees and returns warmth in whatever form it arrives.

*Contemplate:*

**2. Zen Foundation**

This story awakens the principles of *gratitude, humility, right intention, non-attachment, and mindful giving/reception.* Choose the Zen principle this story awakens for you.

*Contemplate:*

**3. Teaching Rooted in the Pali Canon**

Suggested direction: The Buddha taught that only the virtuous know how to be genuinely grateful. Gratitude is a rare and noble quality that opens the heart and honors the giver as much as the gift.

*Contemplate:*

**4. Mindfulness in Practice**

Suggested direction: Today, offer a sincere *thank you* while meditating without expectation—whether to someone close or a stranger. Feel the warmth of appreciation in your own body. Let this be its own blessing, without needing a return.

*Contemplate:*

**5. Reflection Prompts**

- When have I taken kindness for granted—even unintentionally?
- What small act of generosity have I forgotten to acknowledge?
- Do I express gratitude only for flawless gifts, or for sincerity itself?
- How can I become like the cracked cup that still holds light?

*Contemplate:*

**6. Gratitude / Compassion / Simplicity Exercise**

Suggested direction: Write a short message (even just a single line) expressing genuine appreciation to someone you haven't thanked in a while. Do it quietly, without announcing it or expecting anything in return.

*Contemplate:*

**7. Mini-Meditation (1–2 Minutes)**

Sit still. Anchor your attention on a single sensation—your breath at the nostrils or the rise and fall of your chest. Recognize one person and silently send them blessings.

*Contemplate:*

**8. Daily Affirmation**

Suggested affirmation: *"Gratitude fills my cup—even when it has cracks."*

*Contemplate:*

## *Lesson 43: The Bamboo Lesson*

Touba and Junpei clash over a simple meditation cushion under the bamboo grove. Caught in their conflict, Master Shoji leads them to the tallest bamboo and invites them to experience both sides of anger—being struck and striking.

**1. Story Essence**

This story illustrates how quickly the mind can become defensive and violent when clinging to the notion of "mine." Through the bamboo, Shoji teaches the simple truth: all harm cycles back—whether in body, mind, or karma. Compassion begins when we imagine ourselves in the place of the other.

*Contemplate:*

**2. Zen Foundation**

This story awakens the principles of *non-harm (ahiṃsā), empathy, mindful action, humility, and right intention.* Choose the Zen principle this story awakens for you.

*Contemplate:*

**3. Teaching Rooted in the Pali Canon**

Suggested direction: The Buddha taught that "all fear the stick"—reminding us that fear and pain are universal. If we reflect deeply on this, we naturally loosen the impulse to harm others, for we recognize ourselves in them.

*Contemplate:*

**4. Mindfulness in Practice**

Suggested direction: Hold a stick, branch, or pencil lightly in your hand. Reflect on how it feels as both an extension of you and as something that could harm you if used carelessly. Notice your instinct—grasping? Tensing? Softening?

*Contemplate:*

**5. Reflection Prompts**

- In a recent conflict, did I try to win, or did I try to understand?
- When have I used my words or energy like a stick—causing harm?
- What would shift if I paused to feel the other's pain before taking action?
- How can I grow like bamboo—strong, rooted, and unviolent?

*Contemplate:*

**6. Gratitude / Compassion / Simplicity Exercise**

Suggested direction: Offer a silent blessing today to someone you disagree with or have struggled to forgive. Wish them well—not in the mind alone, but from the body, breath, and felt intention.

*Contemplate:*

**7. Mini-Meditation (1–2 Minutes)**

Sit quietly. Place a small bamboo object—or simply a slender green stalk in your front. Gaze softly or visualize the form. Notice its shape, texture, and stillness. Let your attention steady—not clinging, not forcing. When your mind wanders, gently bring it back to the bamboo.

*Contemplate:*

**8. Daily Affirmation**

Suggested affirmation: *"In every exchange, I choose peace over harm."*

*Contemplate:*

## *Lesson 44: The Echo*

Hibiki, a sharp-tongued monk, prided himself on speaking "truth"—until the echoes of his own harshness reflected at him.

**1. Story Essence**

This story reminds us that harsh speech is like a stone thrown into still water—it creates ripples that will eventually return. Those who speak in anger invite more anger.

*Contemplate:*

**2. Zen Foundation**

This story awakens the principles of *right speech, mindfulness in communication, humility, karmic reciprocity, and self-awareness.* Choose the Zen principle this story awakens for you.

*Contemplate:*

**3. Teaching Rooted in the Pali Canon**

Suggested direction: The Buddha taught that harsh speech carries its own punishment, for "malicious talk is the root of suffering." To speak skillfully is to sow quiet and kindness that returns in equal measure.

*Contemplate:*

**4. Mindfulness in Practice**

Suggested direction: Before speaking today, pause and ask: "Will these words nourish or harm? Will they return peace or unrest?" Speak softly, with care, even in small moments. Feel each syllable as an offering.

*Contemplate:*

**5. Reflection Prompts**

- Does my speech create peace or tension in my relationships?
- When have I thrown stones with my words and been surprised by the ripples?
- How can I soften my tone without diluting my truth?
- What would my conversations feel like if each word were chosen like a seed?

*Contemplate:*

**6. Gratitude / Compassion / Simplicity Exercise**

Suggested direction: Choose someone you have spoken sharply to (even in thought). Send them a silent wish of peace or kindness today. Don't expect anything in return—release it like a soft echo into the world.

*Contemplate:*

**7. Mini-Meditation (1–2 Minutes)**

Sit in stillness, with no goal but to be present. Let thoughts, sounds, sensations arise like echoes in an empty hall. Do not follow them, fight them, or judge them. Simply sit, fully awake, without needing to make any adjustments. Simply acknowledge.

*Contemplate:*

**8. Daily Affirmation**

Suggested affirmation: *"May my words be soft, so the echoes return soft."*

*Contemplate:*

## *Lesson 45: The Bamboo Lantern*

Emi lives surrounded by wealth and celebrated teachers—yet feels untouched by their words. Guided by sincerity rather than ceremony, she offers a simple lantern to the night sky, and her true teacher returns, drawn by the silent clarity of her heart.

**1. Story Essence**

This story reminds us that true wisdom is not measured by status or outward offerings, but by the quiet sincerity of the heart. When intention is pure, even the smallest act—a lantern, a breath—can illuminate the farthest path.

*Contemplate:*

**2. Zen Foundation**

This story awakens the principles of *sincerity, faith, mindful devotion, clarity of heart, and the power of quiet presence.* Choose the Zen principle this story awakens for you.

*Contemplate:*

**3. Teaching Rooted in the Pali Canon**

Suggested direction: The Buddha taught that the good—like the Himalayas—are visible even from afar. True goodness cannot be hidden, and sincerity calls forth what is wholesome and wise.

*Contemplate:*

**4. Mindfulness in Practice**

Suggested direction: Light a candle, lamp, or even a soft inner intention today—not to impress anyone else, but to illuminate your own sincerity. Let this act be a quiet offering from the heart, needing no witness or reward.

*Contemplate:*

**5. Reflection Prompts**

- When have I felt clarity without needing confirmation from others?
- How do I distinguish between outward performance and genuine sincerity?
- What is one small act I can offer today that comes from my deepest truth?
- What "bamboo lantern" is waiting in my own life to be released?

*Contemplate:*

**6. Gratitude / Compassion / Simplicity Exercise**

Suggested direction: Offer a silent gesture of devotion today—an unseen gift, a wordless blessing, a quiet act of service (even just a breath of gratitude)—without seeking acknowledgment.

*Contemplate:*

**7. Mini-Meditation (1–2 Minutes)**

Sit still. Focus on the appearance and disappearance of sensations in the body. Observe directly: arising, passing, changing—without judgment or control. See how each sensation, like the lantern, appears briefly, shines, and disappears. Let this reveal impermanence, clarity, and natural peace. Take your time, do not force the revelation.

*Contemplate:*

**8. Daily Affirmation**

Suggested affirmation: *"A sincere heart is a lantern that can be seen from any distance."*

*Contemplate:*

# *Lesson 46: The Lantern of Seeing*

Kaoru is burdened, not by the size of his troubles, but by the constant carrying of them. Through the metaphor of a lantern, his teacher gently reveals the Four Noble Truths: the nature of suffering, its roots, its cessation, and the path that leads to release.

**1. Story Essence**

This story reminds us that even light burdens can become heavy when held without pause. To understand suffering—not avoid or deny it—is the first step. And through recognition, investigation, letting go, and practice, we return to a state of peace.

*Contemplate:*

**2. Zen Foundation**

This story awakens the principles of *right seeing, letting go, insight into suffering, mindful action, and compassionate truth.* Choose the Zen principle this story awakens for you.

*Contemplate:*

**3. Teaching Rooted in the Pali Canon**

Suggested direction: The Buddha described the Four Noble Truths as a guiding lantern in darkness, illuminating what suffering is, its origins, how it ends, and the path to eternal peace.

*Contemplate:*

**4. Mindfulness in Practice**

Suggested direction: Pick up a simple object (a cup, a stone, a book). Hold it gently, then put it down. Notice the relief—not in the absence of weight, but in the act of releasing it. Let this teach you what it means to let go without running away.

*Contemplate:*

**5. Reflection Prompts**

- What burdens do I carry daily, even when I don't have to?
- What expectations or fears do I cling to as "my truth"?
- How could I set down just one burden today—even briefly?
- What does the lantern in this story represent in my own life?

*Contemplate:*

**6. Gratitude / Compassion / Simplicity Exercise**

Suggested direction: Offer one small act of kindness to yourself—placing your hand on your heart, resting without self-judgment, or acknowledging your own effort. Let gratitude soften your grip on perfection.

*Contemplate:*

**7. Mini-Meditation (1–2 Minutes)**

Sit still and bring attention to the breath or a simple sensation (pressure, tingling, warmth). Observe how the sensation arises. Observe how it changes. Observe how it passes. When we recognize that all experience—whether pleasant or painful—is constantly arising and passing away, the grip of suffering loosens. We learn to endure without clinging and release without fear.

*Contemplate:*

**8. Daily Affirmation**

Suggested affirmation: *"I can lay down the lantern. Each breath carries release."*

*Contemplate:*

## *Lesson 47: The Bamboo Path*

Kana seeks peace beyond chanting and scripture. Through a simple bamboo pole, Daisetsu reveals the Noble Eightfold Path—not a doctrine to be memorized, but a way to be walked with every breath, every step, every choice.

**1. Story Essence**

This story reminds us that peace is not found by searching outside ourselves—but by walking the Noble Eightfold Path with sincerity and steadiness. The path may feel narrow, but it is strong enough to carry us through suffering when walked with care.

*Contemplate:*

**2. Zen Foundation**

This story awakens the principles of *right seeing, intentional living, compassion in speech and action, mindful work, inner discipline, and stillness through awareness.* Choose the Zen principle this story awakens for you. *Contemplate:*

**3. Teaching Rooted in the Pali Canon**

Suggested direction: The Buddha taught the Noble Eightfold Path as the middle way—neither indulgence nor rejection, but a path of wisdom, ethics, and concentration that leads to lasting peace.

*Contemplate:*

**4. Mindfulness in Practice**

Suggested direction: Take one simple action today—walking, eating, speaking, writing—and do it with full attention. Let every movement be a step on the path: see clearly, act gently, speak truthfully, breathe mindfully. Notice how presence changes the task.

*Contemplate:*

**5. Reflection Prompts**

- Which step of the Noble Eightfold Path feels most natural to me right now?
- Which step feels most challenging—and why?
- How can I bring the right mindfulness into an ordinary moment?
- When does my speech drift from truth or kindness?
- What kind of work (external or internal) truly nourishes me and others?

*Contemplate:*

**6. Gratitude / Compassion / Simplicity Exercise**

Suggested direction: As you go about your day, consciously choose one step of the path to cultivate—perhaps a kind word (right speech), or a patient response (right effort). End your day by silently thanking yourself for even a single mindful step.

*Contemplate:*

**7. Mini-Meditation (1–2 Minutes)**

Sit in a comfortable posture. Bring awareness to the mind itself. Observe as thoughts, intentions, emotions, and habits arise—noticing whether they align with, or drift from, the path. Is this thought based on compassion or craving? As each mental quality arises, observe its origin, its presence, and its passing without judgment. This is walking the path with eyes open.

*Contemplate:*

**8. Daily Affirmation**

Suggested affirmation: *"Each step, each breath, each choice—this is my path to peace."*

*Contemplate:*

# *Lesson 48: The Lantern in the Cellar*

Itsuki avoided the dark cellar until pain forced him to see it clearly. Only when he lit the space did he discover that what he feared was not a curse—but the simple result of forgetting to bring light.

**1. Story Essence**

This story reminds us that ignorance—inner or outer—is not an enemy, but a shadow waiting for clarity. Avoiding what we refuse to look at only strengthens the fear.

*Contemplate:*

**2. Zen Foundation**

This story awakens the principles *of clear seeing, mindful responsibility, conscience, courage, and gentle self-honesty.* Choose the Zen principle this story awakens for you.

*Contemplate:*

**3. Teaching Rooted in the Pali Canon**

Suggested direction: The Buddha taught that clear knowing (sampajañña)—the awareness of what's truly happening—is the beginning of skillfulness.

*Contemplate:*

**4. Mindfulness in Practice**

Suggested direction: Choose one "cellar" of your life—perhaps a task you've avoided, a feeling you haven't examined, or an old wound you've pushed away. Instead of shutting the door again, bring gentle attention to it. Don't fix everything at once—just turn on the light.

*Contemplate:*

**5. Reflection Prompts**

- What emotional or mental "cellar" have I been avoiding recently?
- What would happen if I looked with curiosity, not criticism?
- What fear or confusion might dissolve once I gain a clearer understanding of the situation?
- What small, compassionate action can I take to bring light into that space today?

*Contemplate:*

**6. Gratitude / Compassion / Simplicity Exercise**

Suggested direction: Write a brief note showing compassion to yourself for having the courage to look into a difficult area of your life. Acknowledge the tender strength it takes to bring light where you once resisted.

*Contemplate:*

**7. Mini-Meditation (1–2 Minutes)**

Sit upright. Bring awareness to an area of discomfort—perhaps pain, confusion, frustration, or fear. Notice the feeling or thought. See it as a "room in the cellar" you are illuminating—not something to fight, but to gently understand. Observe its beginnings, its presence, and its fading using the sensations.

*Contemplate:*

**8. Daily Affirmation**

Suggested affirmation: *"I bring light to what I once feared. With clear seeing, even darkness becomes a friend."*

*Contemplate:*

## *Lesson 49: The Bridge in the Rain*

Taiki walked across the trembling bridge not through bravado, but by leaning into five quiet powers: faith, conscience, prudence, energy, and wisdom.

**1. Story Essence**

The story reminds us that life's bridges often appear unstable, especially when the world around us is in motion. But when we bring trust, clarity, discernment, effort, and understanding to each step, even the most treacherous paths can become walkable.

*Contemplate:*

**2. Zen Foundation**

This story awakens the principles of *trust in the path, ethical awareness, wise restraint, wholehearted effort, and insight,* mirroring the Five Spiritual Powers in practice. Choose the Zen principle this story awakens for you.

*Contemplate:*

**3. Teaching Rooted in the Pali Canon**

Suggested direction: The Buddha taught about pañca-bala, the five powers—faith (saddhā), moral shame (hiri), moral fear or prudence (ottappa), energy (viriya), and wisdom (paññā). These strengths help us navigate life's crossings.

*Contemplate:*

**4. Mindfulness in Practice**

Suggested direction: Think of a "bridge" you are currently afraid to cross—a conversation, a change, a decision. Before stepping forward, pause. Bring faith, conscience, prudence, energy, and wisdom to your heart—like placing steady stones under your feet.

*Contemplate:*

**5. Reflection Prompts**

- What bridge in my life have I been avoiding due to fear or uncertainty?
- Which of the Five Powers do I most need right now?
- How does hesitation feel in my body—and how does courage feel?
- When was the last time I crossed a stormy bridge and arrived safely?

*Contemplate:*

**6. Gratitude / Compassion / Simplicity Exercise**

Suggested direction: Choose one person who has quietly embodied "bridge-crossing courage" in your life. Send them a message of thanks or offer a small act of kindness today in their honor.

*Contemplate:*

**7. Mini-Meditation (1–2 Minutes)**

Sit with your spine straight, allowing your breath to fall into a natural rhythm. Bring your awareness inward and observe the mind just as it is—without attempting to change anything. Notice thoughts arising, changing, and fading. Observe any feelings or intentions that appear—whether pleasant, unpleasant, or neutral—and see them as passing conditions, not as "you" or "yours."

*Contemplate:*

**8. Daily Affirmation**

Suggested affirmation: *"With trust and wisdom, I take each step boldly and gently, even when the path shakes beneath me."*

*Contemplate:*

## *Lesson 50: The Quiet Treasures*

Aya shows Kenshin a different kind of wealth—not coins in chests but inner treasures: faith, virtue, conscience, concern, deep listening, generosity, and discernment. These treasures cannot be burned or stolen; they can only be lived.

**1. Story Essence**

This story reminds us that true security is not found in gold or possessions, but in qualities of heart and mind that no loss can touch. When we cultivate conviction, virtue, compassion, generosity, and insight, we carry a richness that grows the more it's shared.

*Contemplate:*

**2. Zen Foundation**

This story awakens the principles of inner wealth, self-cultivation, generosity, ethical living, and gracious discernment. Choose the Zen principle this story awakens for you.

*Contemplate:*

**3. Teaching Rooted in the Pali Canon**

Suggested direction: The Buddha spoke of the "Seven Noble Treasures" (saddhā, sīla, hiri, ottappa, suta, cāga, paññā)—inner qualities that no fire or flood can destroy.

*Contemplate:*

**4. Mindfulness in Practice**

Suggested direction: Reflect on one inner treasure you already carry—kindness, patience, dedication, honesty—and give it space to grow today. Let it be your quiet wealth.

*Contemplate:*

**5. Reflection Prompts**

- Which of the Seven Treasures do I wish to cultivate more deeply?
- What inner treasure has helped me during difficult times?
- How can I honor these qualities in myself and others?
- If someone could "steal" all my possessions, what treasure would still remain?

*Contemplate:*

**6. Gratitude / Compassion / Simplicity Exercise**

Extend compassion to someone in quiet need—offer a moment of presence, a kind note, a silent wish for their ease. Let your action come from a heart that seeks to understand, not fix or judge. Allow compassion to be your quiet gift.

*Contemplate:*

**7. Mini-Meditation (1–2 Minutes)**

Sit gently. Neither force nor strive. Let breath come and go. Let thoughts rise and fall like leaves on a still pond. Once the mind settles, silently offer compassion starting with yourself: *May I be safe. May I be content. May I rest in ease.*

Extend this to someone you love. Then to someone you struggle with. Finally, to all beings: *May all beings know the peace of these noble treasures.* Return to just sitting—open, present, enough.

*Contemplate:*

**8. Daily Affirmation**

Suggested affirmation: *"I carry the quiet treasures the world cannot take—kindness, clarity, and an open heart."*

*Contemplate:*

## *Recommended Reading and Resources*

For those who wish to go deeper into the practice and understanding of mindfulness, compassion, and Zen teachings, this book humbly acknowledges the wisdom of several foundational works. We encourage readers to explore texts such as:

- Tipitaka, The Pali Canon – Access to Insight: *www.accesstoinsight.org/tipitaka/index.html*
- Book: *For a Future to Be Possible* by Thich Nhat Hanh: *www.plumvillage.org/books/for-a-future-to-be-possible*
- The Dhammapada: *https://www.tipitaka.net/tipitaka/dhp*
- Clear Way Zen: *https://www.clearwayzen.ca/*
- Zen Koans: *https://ashidakim.com/zenkoans*
- Lotus Sutra: *https://www.bdk.or.jp/document/dgtl-dl/dBET_T0262_LotusSutra_2007.pdf*
- *Anguttara Nikaya 8.39: *www.accesstoinsight.org/tipitaka/an/an08/an08.039.than.html*
- **Samyutta Nikaya 56.11: *www.accesstoinsight.org/tipitaka/sn/sn56/sn56.011.than.html*

SCAN ME

**For clickable links and extended readings, scan the QR code.** This collection is lovingly updated from time to time as new resources are added to my reading list—and to your journey.

## *Continuing the Journey*

Hello, Peace Seeker,

Yīng Huā Forest was never just a place. It was a whisper. A quiet vision to welcome those who seek stillness, not in escape, but in presence.

*Whispers of the Zen Forest Workbook* is one small path in that larger forest—a sanctuary where books breathe, tea warms, and silence teaches. Where seekers gather not to become more, but to return home to what has always been.

There is no dogma here. No rigid form. This forest welcomes you—not as a visitor, but as one who belongs. And the path continues—softly, simply, step by step.

**Your Gentle Gifts**

To support your unfolding, you are invited to receive:

- **You Got This** – Mindful Reflections Journal: Gentle prompts to explore your thoughts after each story
- **Mandala Coloring Book:** Creative, soothing designs to relax your mind
- **Audio Tracks:** Calming music and guided narrations for rest and reflection

You're warmly welcome to join our shared space from time to time— **freely offered** for those walking the path with sincerity:

- **30 minutes of meditation** (guided or silent)
- **30 minutes of Dhamma reflection** to deepen understanding.

These invitations are shared through the **Yīng Huā Forest Newsletter**—a quiet leaf in your inbox, carrying reflections, updates, and gentle inspiration.

**Scan the QR code** to receive your gifts and stay connected.

SCAN ME

May your days be spacious.

May your steps be soft.

May your forest always be nearby.

With gratitude and peace,

Sati

## *A Gentle Bow of Thanks*

Hello, Mindful Reader

Thank you for walking with this book—for pausing, breathing, and listening between its pages.

If even one story offered you stillness, or one reflection stirred something true within you, I'm quietly grateful.

If your heart feels moved, I invite you to share a few words in a review. Your review—however simple—helps others find their way here, just as you did. It is like placing a small lantern along the path for someone still searching.

**Scan the QR code** below to leave a review.

SCAN ME

>> Leave a Review on Amazon<<

Thank you for being part of this quiet journey.

May your days unfold with clarity, warmth, and deep peace.

## *About the Author*

**Sati Siroda** is an inspirational author passionate about empowering minds through storytelling. With a knack for weaving simple yet profound tales, Sati inspires readers to embrace their unique potential and navigate life with courage and purpose.

Sati's diverse academic journey—from engineering to education, business, and communication—combined with her extensive travels and time spent in various countries for education, business, and skill development, shapes her holistic storytelling approach. Her experience teaching in schools and universities has further enriched her understanding of young minds, helping her find her path as a storyteller who connects deeply with her audience. Her multifaceted background enables her to connect with readers in relatable and innovative ways.

Her stories are fueled by a belief in the transformative power of narrative. Drawing from her expertise in strategic communication and her love for literature, Sati crafts engaging, uplifting books that instill resilience, emotional intelligence, and self-confidence in her readers. Her mission is clear: to inspire the next generation to dream fearlessly, think critically, and approach life's challenges with creativity and optimism.

As a dedicated meditation practitioner and advocate for mindful living, Sati blends timeless wisdom with gentle insight to help readers reconnect with calm, clarity, and presence in their everyday lives.

Through her heartfelt stories, Sati creates a world where every page becomes a stepping stone toward growth, and every character serves as a guiding light. She warmly invites readers of all ages to embark on a journey of self-love, self-discovery, and empowerment through the enchantment of her books.

Stay connected with Sati Siroda on Instagram: *@SatiSiroda.*

Printed in Dunstable, United Kingdom

79853920R00097